Gorby 2

Audacious Impostor

Ronald V. Knapp

with Adrian Windsor

ISBN: 978-0-9892907-5-3

Publisher
McGregor Wood LLC
14252 Culver Dr. #205A
Irvine, CA 92604

Printed in the United States of America

Contents

Preface

On December 7, 1988, Mikhail Gorbachev, then the Secretary General of the Soviet Union, arrived in New York City with his wife, Raisa, to address the United Nations. Such a gridlock was anticipated in New York City that 6600 police officers were on duty.

His address to the United Nations was one of the most significant speeches of the last half of the twentieth century, because he essentially outlined his plans for troop reductions in Eastern Europe and the withdrawal from Afghanistan, all of this leading to the demise of the Soviet Union and the end of the Cold War.

Ronald Knapp, who had won the Gorbachev Look-Alike Contest in Hollywood a year before, was invited to New York City to do a one-hour show simultaneous with Mikhail Gorbachev's arrival. Fox TV's Gordon Elliott was experimenting with an early version of "*Reality TV*" with a program, *Good Day, New York*. At 7:00 a.m., Ronald Knapp would be knocking on doors in New Jersey, wearing his birthmark, and the TV cameras would capture the reactions of the residents.

New York City was primed for Gorbachev's visit, and Ronald Knapp was a great hit as he knocked on doors and greeted people in their homes in New Jersey. Fox decided to hire a limo and turn Knapp loose on New York, just to see what would happen. It exploded. Not only did the New Yorkers line up to shake his hand and greet him, even Donald Trump came down from his Tower.

On that day Ronald Knapp became infamous as an impostor and became Gorby 2, an identity that has stuck with him in the twenty-five years since that eventful day. The "Afterword" has excerpts from the articles that gave him the "impostor" designation. I was with him in New York City on December 7, 1988. We went to New York for one day, and we ended up staying for eighteen days.

Everywhere we went in Manhattan, Gorby 2 would be stopped on the street and greeted as, "You're the guy who got Trump!" Trump denied that he had been fooled, but the TV cameras told a different story, as recorded on the back cover of Maury Povich's book, *Current Affairs: A Life on the Edge.*

Maury Povich interviewed Ronald Knapp in his program *A Current Affair* on Fox TV. He played footage of Knapp's parade in New York City, of the meeting with Donald Trump in front of Trump Towers, and of the Gorbachev motorcade passing Fox Studio on 67th Street. Fox had stationed Knapp outside the studio, and the motorcade stopped and backed up when they saw Gorby 2 waving at them. Gorby was waving at his own parade.

Maury also played the rock video, "Rock the Wall," that Knapp had envisioned in anticipation that Gorbachev would take down the Berlin Wall. Gorbachev's speech to the United Nations in December of 1988 set the stage for the eventual opening of the Berlin Wall, but the video "Rock the Wall" was made in 1987, two years before the actual Wall came down. Both ARD, West German TV, and TASS, from the Soviet Union, made copies of the video and took them back to play in their countries.

This totally unplanned and serendipitously unfolding "Gorby 2 Parade" in New York City launched Ronald Knapp into a series of amazing encounters and adventures that are recorded in this book. The playing of "Rock the Wall" on Fox TV took him into Europe and the Soviet Union. If there is a basic message within his stories, it is to seize the opportunity and revel in the outcome. Take what life gives you and do something spectacular with it.

Ronald Knapp's sense of humor, "one liners," and pure joy of telling his stories is most often greeted by the question, "Is he telling the truth?" The "truth" is, he is telling the truth. His stories are "off the wall" of most of our experience. The other question frequently asked is, "Weren't you afraid of being assassinated?" He wasn't. He figured that day was as good as any to die. As he stood up in the bubble of the limo and waved to the crowd, I realized that he had done this before, in another lifetime.

As you read the stories in this book, you will come to see that Ronald Knapp has always been a bit of a "trickster." Tricksters play an important part in the folklore and culture of the United States, mischievous and roguish figures identified with cleverness, cunning, deception, subversive humor, and breaking of taboos. The other powerful archetype, the "joker," is portrayed in the Jack of Hearts on the cover of the book.

Fueled by the necessity to survive a turbulent childhood and growing up in Detroit, Ronald Knapp learned to land on his feet and talk himself into and out of situations most of us would avoid. His quick wit and sharp tongue have stood him in good stead and also got him into a whole lot of trouble.

You might say that Knapp's entire life was a preparation for that historic day in New York City when he became labeled as an "impostor." No one could relish more the *persona* he took on after that day than he does. The curious thing is that people take such joy in their encounters with him and in the stories he tells them. He presents life with the dull stuff cut out. Most of us are mired in the "dull stuff," and it's fun to be diverted, even if just for a few minutes.

This is not a book about Ronald Knapp's every day life as a father of five children, as plant manager for McDonnell Douglas overseeing the overhaul and repair of DC9's and DC 10's, as an inventor, business man and entrepreneur. Nor is it even about his exploits as a hunter and long-range fisherman. This is a book about the fun parts and the elements and influences in Ronald Knapp's life that prepared him to seize the moment.

Gorby 2 carries an unlimited supply of business cards that he first made 25 years ago - Gorbachev on one side and him on the other. The first thing he says when he meets a new prospect for conversation is, "Here, let me give you my card." I have never met anyone who delights in telling his stories with undaunted enthusiasm more than Ronald Knapp, Gorby 2. That has been his motivation for the writing of this book. I am here to attest, "He is telling the Truth."

Adrian S. Windsor, Ph.D.

Author of *Seven Tools to Transform Genius into Practical Power*

Introduction

What a gift to be born looking like someone famous and influential. What if I had been born looking like Joseph Stalin instead of Mikhail Gorbachev? What if my double had not been one of the most important political figures of the 20th century? What if Gorbachev had not been *Time Magazine's* "Man of the Year?" How lucky was that - to be in the right place doing the right thing.

Well, guess what: It couldn't have happened if I hadn't been risk taker with honed people skills, a great sense of humor, and quick on my feet. I promise as you read my story, you will be amused, inspired, and moved by how serendipity can emerge when you are ready to seize the moment, make the most of it, and never look back.

Give yourself the gift of enjoying my stories and sharing a glimpse of the power of the moment, the power of the people, and the power of events to shape experience. I hope these stories will give you as much pleasure as the high points have given me. And I hope you will learn that you can be swatted down and get back up to ride the waves of fortune. We are who we are at any moment because of who we are becoming our whole lifetime. Turn the page to begin sharing my outrageous adventures.

Chapter 1

We Never Know What Life Will Hand Us

I Look Like Mikhail Gorbachev

We never know what life is going to hand us, so we need to be prepared to address it head on and to seize the day. If we don't, we are likely to be swallowed up by events and personalities and never to discover the possibilities that are ours for the taking. I truly believe from the moment I was conceived with great gusto in the back seat of a car in 1938, I have had a reckless, defiant attitude.

Very early, in the womb, I knew intuitively that the events swirling around me were of my making and that my very existence was a mobilizing force. The language in those days reflected the attitudes toward the unborn child. My mother "got herself pregnant," and my father "had to marry her." I was running the show!

It made me fiercely independent throughout my childhood. They fought, threatened, divorced, married other people, and I took charge of myself. From my first paper route in the fourth grade, I decided where I would go to school, paid my own tuition, and signed my report cards. My life was not about what they would do for me, but rather, what I would do for myself. It made me an opportunist.

So in the spring of 1987, I'm dropping by to visit my mother, Tresa Callahan Pronesti. As I walk in the door, she waves the *LA Times* front page at me and says, "Your picture is in the newspaper. People are going nuts over this Mikhail Gorbachev. America has fallen in love with this Russian leader, and you really look like him."

And there I was on the front page of the *LA Times*. How amazing was that. A world hungry to end the Cold War had found in Mikhail Gorbachev a man who enjoyed the world stage, who could meet the West more than half way. So, how could I take advantage of this accident of nature that gave us the same face at the same time?

Today we would just Google for answers, but in 1987, the options were slim. My path was the same as many who discover they look like someone important. I sought out Ron Smith's Celebrity Look-Alikes in Hollywood, the one agency that had distinguished itself in this arena. In our initial meeting, they said I needed a glossy photo. They recommended a photographer who, in retrospect, used the $450 he charged me for one picture for his drug habit. It didn't occur to me to shop around. I was an aerospace engineer, not an actor.

Adrian, my adventurous side-kick and cheer-leader, painted on a birthmark. I posed in the same posture of the real Gorbachev on the cover of *Time Magazine*, announcing him "Man of the Year." We juxtaposed that picture next to Gorbachev's *Time Magazine* cover on an 8" x 10" sheet. Twenty-five years later, I am still using that same picture on my business card. Actually, the real Mikhail Gorbachev has aged differently, so I look more like he did then than he does now. You figure that out!

The Gorbachev Look-Alike Contest

Our timing was perfect. The great popularity of Gorbachev prompted the Celebrity Look-Alikes Agency to announce a Gorbachev Look-Alike Contest at Carlos and Charlie's on Sunset Boulevard. Adrian said, "Let's enter you and see how far we can go." We armed ourselves with 100 glossy photos and 500 business cards with the double image and prepared to sweep the judges away.

So here came the contest. We walked in the door, and Adrian started handing out the glossy photos to the judges. There were about 75 contestants from all over the world—Germany, England, France, Russia. The contest winner was supposed to win a bronze statue of himself. Beyond that, Ron Smith of Celebrity

Look-Alikes was drumming up business and creating publicity for himself by sponsoring this at Carlos and Charlie's.

I was the only one who came prepared with pictures, and the judges declared me the winner hands down. Winning the contest was supposed to get me representation by Ron Smith for jobs he could create. The press coverage was exactly what Ron Smith anticipated. The good news is that I was written up in 74 countries and had overnight world-wide publicity.

Wow! That rocked. I thought I was on the way to a great, new Hollywood career. I had borrowed a tape from the Huntington Beach Library on Russian and had taught myself to say hello, and please and thank you. I also made up a few Russian words like "Garagki" (Garage Key) and "Bullshitski," and I felt ready to go.

The Dream

The night after I won the contest, I had a dream. It came to me that Gorbachev was going to prove himself on the world stage by taking down the Berlin Wall. My mind kept going back and forth over the situation. This is what I concluded in my dream:

The USSR was coming out of the Cold War and needed to do business with the world. To convince people he's telling the truth, Gorbachev is going to take down the Berlin Wall as a great gesture of East meets West. Those East Germans have been locked up since the Second

World War, and there may be a new generation of pro-Soviet young people who could act on behalf of the USSR, creating another problem for West Germany.

I was half in and out of sleep, going over in my mind what I knew about Germany and the Second World War and their idea of a super-race. But here in America we had Superman and Wonder Woman in our comic books, and we Americans believed in ourselves and the rights of other countries to have freedom. In my mind, I began to think that if I played the role of Gorbachev, that was a very important role I am playing in America.

The Song "Rock the Wall"

When I woke up in the morning, I said to Adrian, "I know what Gorbachev is going to do. He's going to take down the Berlin Wall. We need to write a song." Neither of us had ever written a song, but we came up with idea of "Rock the Wall," to jump on the rock and roll bandwagon. We had a friend, Jim Mahoney, who played the guitar and sang at a local bar in Peter's Landing in Sunset Beach, and he helped us put our lyrics to music.

> I've been talking for so long
> I thought I'd put my ideas in a song
> After all these years I know it's time
> To tell the world what's on my mind.
>
> I'm gonna rock that wall
> I'm gonna rock that wall

I'm gonna rock that wall
'Til it all comes down.
'Til it all comes down.

When I meet Ronnie face to face
We're going to put a stopper on the old arms race.
Come on everybody, let's give peace a chance;
I'm rocking the wall with my brand new dance!

I'm gonna rock that wall
I'm gonna rock that wall
I'm gonna rock that wall
'Til it all comes down.
'Til it all comes down.

Put a wall here, put a wall there,
Sometimes the reasons aren't even clear.
We put 'em up, we can take 'em down
Zamir, the Premier is coming to town.

I'm gonna rock that wall
I'm gonna rock that wall
I'm gonna rock that wall
'Til it all comes down.
'Til it all comes down.

Whoa! Whoa! (Wall comes down!)

I can do the Twist, I can do the Boogie,
I can do the Shimmy, Boogie, Woogie, Woogie.
I'm goin' on, down to the ranch
To teach Mr. Ronnie how to do my dance.

I'm gonna rock that wall
I'm gonna rock that wall
I'm gonna rock that wall
'Til it all comes down.
'Til it all comes down.

Zamir, the Premier, is coming to town.
Peace, Peace is coming down.
Zamir, the Premier, is coming to town.
Peace, Peace is coming down.

I'm gonna rock that wall
I'm gonna rock that wall
I'm gonna rock that wall
'Til it all comes down.
'Til it all comes down.

It's coming down, it's coming down.
It's coming down, it's coming down.

I'm gonna rock that wall
I'm gonna rock that wall
I'm gonna rock that wall
'Til it all comes down.

We made a tape of the song with Jim Mahoney on the guitar, and we began carrying it around with us, playing it for anyone who would listen. One afternoon we were on a visit to a property with a young man who worked for a billion dollar Japanese development firm. This was the hey day of the Japanese purchase of U.S. properties, and they were gobbling up high-rises and hotels.

He listened to our song in the car, and he liked it. He took us up to the penthouse of a high rise in Beverly Hills, to what we thought was his apartment and office. The Secretary who greeted us seemed tense about our being there. As events played out, we recalled the uneasiness of the Secretary and realized that he was pretending that this was his personal space.

We had shared with him the idea that this song could be used for a rock video. No decision was made on this first meeting, but he eventually came to the decision to be our financial partner to make the video. He would be the producer, and he found someone in Hollywood who could direct it. After a series of meetings, we came up with the script and story board.

The Video "Rock the Wall"

The director began the construction of a maze that Gorby would walk through at the beginning, accompanied by Russian military security. We planned to film it on a Saturday, and we called everyone we knew to get them to come and be in the video. We were amazed how many people showed up for the filming.

In this video, Gorby and Reagan try a series of things to take down the wall - a sledge-hammer, a jack-hammer, and finally I ride a construction ball through the Berlin Wall. When the wall opens up, I come bursting through the wall doing the Gorbachev Rock, followed by about

200 friends we recruited, including look-alikes for Stevie Wonder, Pope John Paul, Susan Sarandon and Angelina. It was a massive celebration, and we were all euphoric.

We made the video two years before the Berlin Wall came down. It still is amazing that what happens in the video, what we portrayed, is exactly what happened at the real Berlin Wall. My dream was just one of many times in my life when I have been able to tell the future. Our decision to act on the dream and push ahead to make the 3.5 minute video, however, proved costly and harrowing. Our financial partner paid the director $75,000. The making of the video required more time than calculated, and the director ran up the price with overtime. We did not have the additional money.

Adrian had signed real estate commission agreements for properties we expected to sell. We were willing to put the commissions up as collateral. The director accepted that, verbally, and the production team completed the video. There was great enthusiasm on the set, and we were carried forward by the momentum of the event.

We were so naive about the ways of Hollywood. We didn't question whether people really were who they appeared to be, and we didn't know enough about production to question the overtime cost. We were so eager to make the video, that was all we could see. If we hadn't been like that, the video would never have been made. It caused us a "world of grief."

A Dream Becomes a Nightmare

The real estate deals never closed, so there was no commission. Then the director sued us for $10,000,000. It was his intention to tap into the deep pockets of the company our financial partner worked for. The lawyer who was supposed to be representing us, had us sign a document saying the partner had not represented that his company was involved.

This was actually not the truth, because he had led us to believe the penthouse office was his apartment. We were misled by the young man and misled by the lawyer. We shouldn't have signed it. My dream had turned into a nightmare. The video we expected to spring on the world was tied up in court for almost a year.

In early December of 1988, the judge who tried the case awarded the video to us, saying that we were the only ones who could do anything with it. The partner had no money, we had no money, and the only possible outcome would be for "Gorby 2" to promote it.

By then, I had become so identified with Mikhail Gorbachev that most people knew me by Gorby. If Adrian mentioned "Ron," they would say, "Who's he?" This was the beginning of a series of serendipitous events.

Grabbing for Gigs

While the video was tied up in court, I did begin to do a few Gorby Look-Alike gigs. People think Celebrity

Look-Alikes get paid big money, and some of them may, but that was not my experience. When you are "news," you don't get paid at all. Most of my appearances over the past 25 years have been charity donations. It was always a hassle to get paid.

I would do the job, and then I would wait. The agency took the bulk of the money and paid me my pittance when they got around to it.

At one point I asked my brother, Jim, to create a phony gig at a county fair for me, just so I could get paid for past appearances. He called and sold the county fair job to an agent with the event paying the agent $12,000 for my appearance. The agent offered me $500. I accepted under the condition that I would get paid for the last three jobs I had done. It took four days for the agent to pay up. After I finally got my money, my brother cancelled the county fair event.

The Car of the Year for the Man of the Year

One of the most striking gigs took place in New York City. Adrian and I were in Florida for her parents' 50th Wedding Anniversary when I got a phone call to come to New York City as Gorby for the Pontiac Dealers big annual meeting. The Pontiac Grand Prix had been named the "Car of the Year." *Time Magazine*, the year before, had named Gorbachev, "The Man of the Year." The Pontiac dealers thought it would be a great idea for "The Man of the Year" to receive "The Car of the Year" and to publicize the event.

Adrian's father put the plane ticket on his credit card, and I boarded a plane in Fort Myers early in the morning to head for New York City. I was wearing my birth mark. Adrian paints it on with the kit used for black eyes in movie make-up. The people on the plane were looking at me and whispering to each other. The stewardess finally came over and said, "Are you Mr. Gorbachev? Everyone is asking."

I replied, "Shh, don't tell anybody." She, of course, told the captain, and he announced through the speaker that Mr. Gorbachev was on the plane.

I said, "Hello, How are you?" in Russian to the man sitting next to me.

He said, "I'm sorry, Sir. I do not speak your language."

I said, "Well, I can speak English." And we began our conversation. It turned out that he was the President of Prudential Insurance. He asked what I was doing, and I told him I was on my way to receive "The Car of the Year." He asked who was meeting me at the airport, and I said "Someone named Larry."

He said, "No, I am going to send you to that event in my limousine." When we got off the plane, his limo was waiting, and I got in.

So, you can imagine what happened when I arrived. The Pontiac dealers were all outside by the curb, and I got out of the limo, very much projecting the image of the real thing. They all stood in line to shake my hand. I spoke Russian to them.

The young man who represented the Public Relations Firm that planned the event had been in Washington, D.C. when Gorbachev was there. Gorbachev had gone out of his limo and into the street to shake hands with people. This man, Tom Gionocchio, was impressed by how much I looked like the real Gorbachev and how well I carried this off.

"The Car of the Year" was in a huge closed box sitting on the ground next to a Pontiac dealership overlooking the water, wrapped and decorated with a big ribbon. When the box was opened and the car was driven out, the media who were filming the event said, "Do something Russian." So, I took off my shoe and beat on the hood of the car. Nikita Kruschev had done that on a visit to address the United Nations when he was Secretary General of the Soviet Union. The car dealers loved it and applauded. Gorby shook hands, took pictures, and personally greeted all of the 600 Pontiac dealers. I still occasionally meet a dealer who was there.

After the event, the public relations firm took me to Carnegie's Deli for lunch. It was packed with people. A big mouth Irishman yelled out, "Gorby has arrived." They all shook hands with me. The owner of the Deli said he would personally make a pastrami sandwich for me. It was the biggest sandwich I have ever seen. I could only eat half of it, and I took the other half back to Florida for Adrian. This was a very special moment for me. The owner took pictures with me. He was vigorous and appeared to be in good health. The next day he died of natural causes.

Gorbachev Is Coming to Town

Tom Gionnochio left the public relations firm and moved on to Fox TV. He remembered me.

In December of 1988, the day before Raisa and Mikhail Gorbachev were scheduled to arrive in New York City for Gorbachev to address the United Nations, Tom called Adrian.

He said, "Are you guys coming to New York for Gorbachev's visit?"

Adrian said "We hadn't planned to, but what do you have in mind?

He said, "Gordon Elliott has a TV show called *Good Day, New York* where he goes to people's houses at 7:00 a.m. unexpectedly, just knocking on the door. We thought it would be fun to take Gorbachev to New Jersey at 7:00 a.m. the day he is arriving in New York to see what will happen." This was "Reality TV" long before Reality TV.

Jack Stovall, the President of Best Western International, had befriended us. He thought I was a potential source of income, and he had an entrepreneurial spirit. His father had been one of the original 33 supporters of Walt Disney, had founded Stovall Inns and founded Best Western International. Jack had been a scout for the Rams, founded the Sports Clinic in Anaheim, and was an early promoter of the Super Bowl when it first became big. We didn't have the money for the plane ticket. He put the ticket on his credit card, and we left LAX at 11:00 p.m. to take the Red Eye to New Jersey.

Chapter 2

My Parade in New York City

Gorby in New Jersey

We arrived at Kennedy Airport at 6:00 a.m. and were hustled off to New Jersey. We were greeted by Gordon Elliott and the Fox TV crew. At 7:00 a.m., I began knocking on doors. At the first house, a little boy looked out of the door window and called his mother: "Ma, Ma, the man that runs Russia is at our front door."

The mother, in her housecoat and curlers, came to the front door and said, "You're the most important person who ever came to our front door."

At the next house, the mother and father both came to the door and invited me into the kitchen. They called their neighbors to come over and meet me, and they offered me breakfast. I didn't dare eat. They pretty much took care of my limited vocabulary: Good morning (Dobroe utro), How are you? (Kak vasi dela?),

Thank you (Spasibo), You're welcome (Pozalujsta), Pleased to meet you (Prijatno poznakomitsa),Good-by (Do svidanija). The Fox crew hustled me out of there before I blew my cover.

The high point of this show was when a truck driver screeched to a halt in the middle of the street. He jumped out of his big truck, plugged up the traffic, horns tooting. He turned around and said "Fungula" to the traffic . He turned to me and said, "I love you, Mr. Gorbachev, but I can't speak Russian. I'm Italian,"

I said, "Gorbachev can sing in Italian," and I sang:

> *"C'na luna mezz'u mare*
>
> *Mamma mia m'a maritare"*

The truck driver started to cry! When Fox TV saw what an impact I was making on the people of New Jersey, they said, "Let's get a limo and turn this guy loose on New York to see what happens."

Only in Manhattan

What ensued could only take place in Manhattan because it is so dense. The whole city was wired for the Gorbachev visit. It was on the news continually. Pictures of Raisa and Mikhail Gorbachev were on every television network and had been for days. This was Christmas time, and a song had been written to the tune of "Santa Claus Is Coming to Town."

"You'd better watch out, you'd better not cry. You'd better stay home, I'm telling you why: Gorbachev is coming to town."

This tune accompanied broadcasts of the entrance of Raisa and Mikhail Sergeyevich Gorbachev into New York from their plane as they were descending the stairs. It was on every TV network.

The limos arrived, and Gorby 2 began his own motorcade down the streets of Manhattan. I stood up in the bubble and waved to the crowds as we progressed. The New York cops came alongside on their motorcycles. They wanted to know: "Where is your Security?"

Gorby responded, "I don't need Security. I'm from Detroit."

The Irish cop said, "Christ, we need the Security." This was an Irish officer, O'Brian.

Gorby said, "My mother was a Callahan!"

The Gorbachev motorcade was on one street, and we were on another. The cops were calling each other, puzzled about the whole thing. There were more than 6000 cops on duty this day. The group with the Gorbachev motorcade was saying, "We've got Gorbachev."

And the group with me was saying, "We've got Gorbachev. Hell with you!"

Finally, the ones with me concluded, "You keep yours. We'll keep ours!"

They said to me, "You could be in danger."

And I replied, "This would be as good a day as any to die."

O'Brian said, "He's from Detroit."

And the other officers said, "Oh, shit!"

They took me to Bloomingdale's, and I got out of the limo and started shaking hands. Some iron workers who were up on top of a building called out. "What about the workers?"

I yelled back, "Come on down."

They did - about two hundred of them. I shook hands with every one of them. I wore my hand out. All I could think of was in both Russia and the United States, the workers, the people make this land go: the unions, the truckers, the crane operators, and the guy with the shovel in his hand, the workers. I shook hands with every one of them with my firmest hand shake.

One worker said, "This is a real leader. He gets out with the people and shakes your hand."

Gordon Elliott guided me through the crowds, and the cameras from Fox TV followed us. A Santa Claus was on the street ringing a bell. He wanted to take a picture with me. A crowd of about 200 people gathered. Santa pulled down his beard and kissed me on the head. He had no teeth. I told him, "I used to play Santa Claus, but now I'm a Communist trying to make a living." In fact, I played Santa Claus for 47 years.

We went to Times Square, and a man came out of the crowd with a hat on that made him look like he came out of the '40's. He said, "Mr. Gorbachev, I am from Poland" in a heavy accent. "I would like to buy you a hot dog."

I said, "What is this thing, hot dog? Do the Amerikanskis eat dogs?" Everyone laughed.

He said, "You don't understand. No dog in the bun, just meat from a cow and a pig in a roll, with mustard, sauerkraut, pickles, and tomatoes."

He goes up to the nearby wagon and buys a giant hot dog. People are gathering fast to watch me eat. The hot dog is so big my mouth barely goes around it. I took a bite slowly and then jumped on one foot and said in broken English: "This is a miracle. Americanskis eat dog, and it is so good."

Everyone cheered, about 300 people, like mana from heaven had just arrived. I had yellow mustard all over my mouth. Then I took a bite of polish pickle. I said, "It's so good, tomorrow we will attack Poland and take all of the pickles.

The crowd laughed and the Polish guy was happy. He said, "We just beat Russia with Polish pickles."

I was famished. When we got off the plane, we went straight to New Jersey without stopping for breakfast. This was my first food since we had left Los Angeles the night before. I was struck by the intense curiosity of the crowd and the warmth of their welcome.

It was time to move on. I loved standing up in the bubble of the limo, waving to the crowd. Adrian said that I must have had a past life in Rome as a Caesar, it came so naturally to me. Where else but in New York City could such a thing happen. People were in the streets everywhere, and the public enthusiasm for this momentous day in history made them eager to be a part of it.

Chapter 3

We Got Donald Trump

Trump Tower

The crowning moment came when we pulled up to Trump Tower. At least 5000 people were gathered outside the tower when I rode up, standing up in the bubble, waving to the crowd.

Some Policemen came up on horseback. We were plugging up the street, and the sirens were blowing. I thought: "All of this excitement over one Communist."

Someone yelled, "It's Gorbachev!" Then they all came running. I was shaking hands and signing autographs as fast as I could.

Then the manager of the Trump Tower came up to the limo and said, "Please, don't leave. Please don't leave. Donald Trump is coming down, Donald Trump is coming down."

I turned my back on him to wave to the crowd as Donald Trump rushed forward. It turned out that Trump had given an invitation to Raisa and Mikhail to come to a private dinner at Trump Tower. They had refused the invitation, saying that they had too many public appearances and obligations already arranged during their visit to New York.

So, that is why "The Donald" said to me, "I heard. I couldn't be more happy to see you. I'm sorry we couldn't make my schedule meet yours."

The TV cameras from Fox were recording this encounter and scanning the crowd. Donald Trump really meant was he was saying. I was thinking to myself what a big ham I was and that if they ever found out, they would skin me alive.

I spoke to Donald Trump with the Russian I learned from a tape in the Huntington Beach library. I said, "Hello! (Zravstvujte)," "How are you? (Kak vasi dela)?"

And then, I don't know what provoked this, I said "I like your tie." He was wearing a red tie.

Gordon Elliott said, "Mr. Secretary, we had better be going."

Donald Trump, getting it for the first time, said, "Have a good time," as I climbed back into the limo.

Gordon Elliott winked at the camera and said, "I think he worked it out."

The people from Fox were ecstatic. They were all yelling, "We got Donald Trump! We got Donald Trump!"

A Current Affair: Rock the Wall on Air

Who would have thought such a thing could happen, totally serendipitously, totally without planning. We went from Trump Tower to the Fox studio, and we got there just before the real Gorbachev motorcade passed by on the way to the Soviet Mission.

The News Team positioned me right outside the door of Fox Studio. There I was, waving to the motorcade. It stopped and backed up to see me, and the crew got the video for the evening news. The announcement was: "The Gorbachev motorcade stopped in front of the Fox Studio and backed up to see their own Gorbachev waving at them from the curb. But it wasn't Gorbachev at all, but his double, an actor from Los Angeles. Only in New York!"

Maury Povich had a 5:00 p.m. newscast on Fox every afternoon, *A Current Affair*. He played the footage in front of Trump Tower and in front of Fox Studio, and then he brought me on the air for an interview. He asked me, "What else do you have up your sleeve?"

I pulled out the video, "Rock the Wall," and said, "I just got this out of court."

He played it on the air. So, on the air for the first time is "Rock the Wall," taking down the Berlin Wall two years before the wall came down. No one believed us when we wrote the song and made the video. Maury said, "How do you know the Wall is coming down?"

I said, "Maury, this came to me in a dream. Gorby is going to do this to prove he is a good guy from the East, to convince the West that he's a peace maker. "

2200 Media Write-Ups

When I went into Fox TV the next day, they had a stream of media write-ups spread across the floor, 2200 in one day. We raised the Nielson rating for Fox seven points in that one day. It was just the beginning of attention from the media. On a tour of NBC a few weeks later, the group in front of us all wanted to shake my hand, and the same thing happened when we went into the newsroom.

The *L.A. Times* published my picture with the headline "He Could Cause Tremblin in the Kremlin." The *Orange County Register* featured the headline: "Huntington Beach Man a Chip off the Communist Block." *Gente, the People's Magazine* in Milan, Italy, carried a nine-page story on me. The author, Nicoletta Sipos, interviewed me for three hours on the telephone for the article.

She said, "You do everything with humor."

I said, "I do. It will take you through life and beyond."

Maury Povich's *Current Affairs* Back Cover

When Maury Povich wrote his Memoir of his days at Fox in his book, *Current Affairs: A Life on the Edge*, he wrote about this incident and me. My mother was the first to discover it, and she called me and said, "You're on the back cover of Maury Povich's new book, *Current Affairs*, and he wrote three pages about you." This is what he said on the back cover:

In December 1988, Mikhail Gorbachev was in New York and had been invited to visit the lavish Trump Tower on Fifth Avenue, but time was tight, and Gorbachev canceled. It was a shattering disappointment for a man of Trump's ego.

…Gordon Elliott, our reporter, hired a stretch limousine and two knockout models. Between them he put Ronald V. Knapp, an actor and rubber salesman who had won a Gorbachev lookalike contest. And off they went down Fifth Avenue. . . .

Meanwhile, Donald Trump had been alerted. Aides had rushed to his office and reported that the head of the Soviet Union was about to keep his historic rendezvous. . . . .Trump hurried down and fought his way through the wedge of phony security people. 'Good to see you again,' Trump said with that famous Trump smile. Donald was actually blushing, caught up in the bigness of the moment. Finally, because he was not a complete fool, Donald noticed something odd. . . . .Something whispered to him that the head of all the Russians would not travel openly around New York City.

Afterward, Trump issued formal statements that he had known all along it was not the real Gorbachev, that he was such a good sport he had gone along with the joke. But if you watched the tape and saw the color leave his face with pale comprehension you could see that he had been completely and utterly fooled.

From CURRENT AFFAIRS: A LIFE ON THE EDGE BY MAURY POVICH, copyright 1991 by Maury Povich. Used by permission of G.P. Putnam's Sons, a division of Penguin Group (USA) Inc.

Video Released on the World

The ramifications of playing the video were enormous. Late that night both ARD, West German TV, and Soviet TV contacted me. They wanted copies of the video. I let each of them borrow the video to make copies in the PAL format for their countries. The video, made in 1987, was played in Germany and the Soviet Union a full year before the actual Berlin Wall came down.

We know it influenced the climate of opinion. We have met people from Europe regularly over the years who saw it. We were in an art gallery in Fashion Island in 2010. We went into a little nook to view a painting of the city streets of Paris. The woman working there came up to us and said, "That painting is the work of a Russian artist."

I said a few words in Russian to her and gave her my card.

She said, "I know you. I saw your video. I laughed so hard I fell off the couch and rolled on the floor."

I said, "Where were you?" She was Iranian.

And she said, "I was living in Azerbaijan." And then she said, "Your picture was actually on the billboards and in the buses and taxi cabs."

And I said, "What did it say?"

She replied, "The New Russia!"

Best Western Rejection

Another incident occurred with Jack Stovall, who was President of Best Western International. They were having a big meeting in Amsterdam. At the time, Best Western was running a series of advertisements featuring Yakov Smirnoff about the King Size beds in their motels. It was actually a pretty stupid ad.

I said to Jack, "Why don't you use Gorby 2 in your ads?"

He said, "I'll run it past the owners."

So, he took the video to his meeting in Amsterdam and played it for these motel owners from all over the world. When he came back, he said, "You really made a fool out of me. They told me the Wall isn't coming down for a hundred years."

When Jack retired as President of Best Western, his wife, Sarah, invited me to come to the meeting in Phoenix, Arizona as a surprise. This was after the Berlin Wall had come down. There were about 3000 people in the room, and Jack was up on the platform behind the podium when I walked into the auditorium, wearing the birth mark. Jack was stunned.

He brought me up on stage, introduced me as Gorby 2 and mentioned to the group that they had seen my video in Amsterdam. Jack also announced, "I met with the Government about Gorby in San Diego. They just love Gorby!" (This was my first indication Jack had been getting paid to report on me by the Bush administration.)

The Best Western people rose and gave me a standing ovation. After the ceremony, it took me half an hour to make my way to the restroom. Everyone there wanted to shake my hand. It didn't take a hundred years.

Chapter 4

Eighteen Days in New York City

Soviet Trade Show at the Jacob Javitz Center

We went to New York City for one day to do *Good Day New York*. We ended up staying for 18. The Gorbachev visit was regarded by the Soviet Union as a way for them to showcase their goods, and a huge trade show was opening at the Jacob Javitz Center. The Russians had sent their most beautiful models to wear their elegant furs. They had Russian cars, Russian jewelry, Russian clothes. Gorbachev was scheduled to open that Trade Show. It turned out, however, that this was one of many scheduled appearances that had to be cancelled.

An earthquake took place in Armenia right after Gorbachev addressed the United Nations, and Raisa and Mikhail returned swiftly to their country to deal with the crisis. The planners of the Trade Show came to me and asked if I would take the place of the real Gorby.

I said, "What an honor. I accept."

They picked us up in a limo and drove us to the Jacob Javitz Center where the media had gathered for the grand opening. They flashed pictures of me as I emerged from the car. They had a name tag all prepared for me that said "Mikhail Gorbachev." I took pictures with the gorgeous models in their furs, and I got to kiss every one of them.

It was apparent that the sales representatives at the show had absolutely no knowledge of marketing. The first incident was with the Zil, the Russian car that they had on display.

I said to the man standing in front of it, "The keys, please."

He said, "I don't have the keys. We left them in Moscow."

I said, "How are you going to sell the Amerikanskis the car?"

He said, "I'm sorry," and ducked as if he thought he might get socked.

And I said, "I am going to send you to Siberia."

He said, "What will I do there?"

And I replied, "You will sell cars."

He said, "Cars don't sell in Siberia."

So I said, "Then you are going to grow cucumbers. Do cucumbers grow in Siberia?"

He said, "Niet, Gorby."

It was literally impossible to get any of the Russians to hand out a business card. I was moving around the show, meeting people, shaking hands, laughing with them. A man in a fine suit came up to me and said, "I can't believe what you are doing with these Russians. Could you help me get a business card from that big one over there?"

I went up to the Russian and scolded him for not giving out his business card.

I said, "We have no secrets. Business card, please." He handed it over.

Gratefully, the man thanked me and then said:

"I own a chain of pizza restaurants called "Old Chicago," and one is in Washington, D.C. We are doing a fund raiser for Leukemia during the week of George Bush's Inauguration. Would you be willing to come as Gorby for that event?"

I said, "I would be delighted!"

He agreed to pay airfare for Adrian and me, to pay me for the event, and to provide hotel and a per diem for food and expenses. How great was that! I was finally getting paid! This was seizing the moment. In addition, he was giving us two tickets to the Inaugural Ball. More about that later.

You're the Guy Who Got Trump

The Trade Show was just the beginning of the planned events where I took the real Gorby's place. When we walked down the streets in Manhattan, people would stop me and say, "You're the guy who got Trump!"

One evening, we were going around the corner near the Marriott Hotel when we came upon a theater with the opening of *The Rain Man*. Shaun Connery was in a large crowd of people. He said, "Gorby, Gorby, come over here. We've known each other a long time." The manager of the theater wanted his picture with both of us. Actually, we attended the cast party for *Red October*.

We finally escaped the crowd and headed over to the Marriott Hotel. As we walked in, the Bus Boy said, "Gorby, I've got a party for you - Russian Vodka, A Stolichnaya Party."

We entered the room of the party and stole the show, They took pictures of me holding up a bottle of Stoly. It made the front page of Russian news: "Gorby drinks the best: Stolichynaya."

Months later, I did a job for the Stoly competitor, Smirnoff, promoting a new vodka, Tarkhuna, from Belise, Soviet Georgia. It was green and never caught on. We did 66 parties all up the coast of California. I would arrive at a bar in a limo with four beautiful models, walk into the bar and yell: "Gorby's here. The drinks are on the house."

In San Jose we stopped at a bar and several Marines were outside the door. I asked why they didn't go in, and they said they couldn't afford the cover charge. Just then the manager came out, and I said, "Unless you let these Marines come in, I'm canceling the visit."

The manager said, "OK," and the Marines gave a big cheer for Gorbachev. One Marine took a medal off from his uniform and gave it to me, thanking me for solving their problem.

I said, "The U.S. Army just came to your defense."

The Marines said, "God bless the Army, Mr. Gorbachev."

But back to New York. One morning a gentleman wearing an overcoat and a hat stopped us. He said, "You're the guy who got Trump! You have given me so much pleasure watching you on television this week, that I want to do something for you. I own a limo company, and I will make a limo and driver available for you any time you need it. It will be on me!"

"Wow!" I said. "Thank you so much."

Brighton Beach Party

We took him up on it, and were especially grateful when we attended a party in Brighton Beach that had been planned for Gorbachev. Brighton Beach is a community close to New York City where many

‐

Russian immigrants have settled. There were 900 people attending this party. As is the Russian habit, it really didn't get started until 11:00 p.m. We had arrived at 9:00 p.m. and saw the tables all set up as they do at their parties. In front of Gorby's place at the head table were a bottle of vodka and a bottle of brandy. Bottles of vodka and brandy lined the tables, with one every few places.

I said to Adrian, "Yo, Adrian, hide this bottle of vodka in your dress, take it to the restroom, pour out the vodka, and fill it full of water."

What a good idea! They stood up all night long, time after time, toasting Gorbachev.

About 2:30 a.m., one of the men at our table said, "Boy, that Gorby, he can really drink."

One of the first people to arrive at the party after us was a man who had written a book on *How to Do Business with the Soviet Union*. He said he thought that perhaps I would like to do seminars with him.

Adrian said "He's not the seminar type."

As the Russians began arriving, one of them asked, "Who is that man?"

I said, "He wrote a book about doing business in Russia."

They said, "Do we like the book, Gorby?"

I said, "Niet."

So they said, "Is it all right to throw him out?"

And I said, "Yes." So they did.

It's good thing we had the limo and driver there waiting for us. That party didn't end until 5:30 a.m.

TV Appearances in New York City

Gordon Elliott featured me on *Good Day, New York* every morning for a week, doing unexpected things. One morning we visited a home in New Jersey with a high school band. Another morning I went roller skating down 57th Street in front of Hammacher Schlemmer. Every time I did something, I attracted large crowds of people who wanted to shake hands with the "Guy Who Got Trump." We didn't realize that Fox resented anything else we did while we were in the City.

It came to a head the morning I was asked to be on *Regis and Kathy Lee*. ABC sent their limo to pick me up at 7:30 a.m. for the show which aired at 9:00 a.m. Gordon Elliott would not let me leave. The limo driver kept saying we had to go and had frantic calls from the ABC studio because we weren't there yet.

We got to ABC after 9:00 a.m. The show began at 9:00 a.m. They rushed us in. It affected the whole interview because Kathy Lee was so furious about my late arrival and was consequently stand-offish and hostile. We didn't realize until later the game that Fox had been playing with us.

One of my big regrets came with *Saturday Night Live*. They called me at Fox the day of the parade and wanted me on the show that Saturday. At that time, Jack Stovall was attempting to organize my activities from Los Angeles. He wanted them to pay me, and they said, "No." In retrospect the publicity from it would have been priceless. How stupid was that! The truth is that things happened so fast after the Trump incident, we were out of control.

TASS and ARD

Soviet TV came and got me to spend time with them. We were taken into the Soviet headquarters filled with computers.

When I walked into the room, they said, "Those are our secrets."

I said, "We know all about your secrets."

They laughed.

The writing was all in Cyrillic, and we couldn't read a word. We went into a small room in the back to chat. Most of them spoke English. The subject turned to Christmas and St. Nicholas, who was Russian. Adrian began to talk about my playing Santa Claus, which I did for 47 years. She asked me to do my "Ho, Ho, Ho," which is very loud, and it scared them all. They came running out of their offices.

ARD, West German Television, spent an entire day with
me, taking me around NYC in a limo and taping my
encounters with people. We went to the Empire State
Building, to Wall Street, to the Metropolitan Museum
of Art, to the Russian Tea Room. They wanted to get me
in trouble to create an incident with negative publicity,
just to give their broadcast a little "razzel dazzle."

Finally, we ended up in Harlem. The crowd we attracted
was huge, and they truly believed I was actually
Gorbachev. Many of them had big wads of cash. The
first one to have me sign money came with a dollar
bill. The next guy wanted to "up" his with a $20. Then
they were rushing me, bringing $100 bills for me to
sign. - obviously drug money. I said, "Why don't I just
give you a receipt?" Adrian noticed that one of them
was suspicious that I wasn't the real thing, and she told
ARD we had to get out of there.

Navigating Danger

We barely made it into the limo before the crowd
began to turn against us. That was my most dangerous
moment in New York City. There were several times
during the 18 days when it was touch and go. I would
stand in the door of a restaurant, hold up my arms, and
yell, "Gorbachev has arrived."

Inevitably the owner would invite us in for a free meal.
Often people would come to us and tell us their stories

about their past in the Old Country. Adrian was always very good about knowing intuitively when we needed to leave before we broke the spell. These people were believers!

One possible danger, I did escape. We went into a bar in New York City, and I was tapped on the shoulder by a man who was one of four Federal Agents gathered there.

He said, "How about joining the FBI?"

I said, "That takes a Heineken." He bought a Heineken for Adrian and me.

We drank that, and he said, "So, what do you think about it?"

And I said "It takes two Heinekens." So, he bought another round,

Then he said, "Ok, Gorby, will you join the force?"

I said, "Niet."

A few years ago, we were amazed when Robert Hanson, the Soviet spy who killed 35 agents, was arrested. We recognized his picture. He was the man who asked me to join the FBI. Robert Hanson got life in prison.

Our trip to Soviet TV, TASS, and my refusal to join the FBI may have triggered the interest our government had in tapping our phone for three years and assigning agents to track us. I gave the real Gorbachev a tremendous amount of free publicity, and our government didn't know who hired me. The truth is, the whole event was spontaneous, but who would have believed that could happen. We counted 27 agents on our trail over a three year period.

A few years ago, I was walking across a park in Dana Point, California. A man stopped me and said, "I know you. I followed you for three years for the CIA. You were clean as a pin. They finally took me off your case when they sent me to Costa Rica."

I didn't even remember seeing him before. I said, "We guessed there must have been 27 agents writing reports on us. Is that accurate?"

He said, "That's about right."

That reminded me of when I went to Jack Stovall's retirement in Phoenix, and he told the audience he had met with agents in San Diego. He also told them I was entirely clean. It took us quite a while to figure out that Jack was an agent, too, assigned to watch us and to keep the lid on us.

Chapter 5

George Walker Bush Inauguration

The Leukemia Ball

The gentleman from the Russian Trade Show at the Jacob Javitz Center was as good as his word. He even came through with the tickets to the Inaugural Ball. Jack Stovall decided to go with us and magically produced two tickets to the Inaugural Ball for himself. He said it was from a source in Las Vegas. It made sense, when we finally figured out he was an agent. His tickets came from our government. His son, Sammy, came along, too. Jack booked rooms for us at a Best Western in Maryland, about 20 miles from Washington, D.C., and he rented a car to drive us back and forth.

The Inauguration was a week-long series of multiple events. We attended a U.S. Senate party where each senator had a booth. I was wearing my birth mark, and they invited me to their booths to take pictures with them. They showered me with gifts from the state they represented. Several of them gave us bottles of wine. We were up to four shopping bags, and Jack and Adrian were loaded down.

Finally Jack said, "I'm sick and tired of being your beast of burden and carrying all your wine."

The truth is, he was sick and tired of my getting all of the attention. He was accustomed to being the center of attention himself.

The Leukemia Ball was the night before the Inauguration and the Inaugural Ball. They picked Adrian and me up in a limo, and we arrived on site with the media flashing their cameras. Two of the men in front of the auditorium were from Radio Station WXYZ in Detroit. They loved the fact that Gorby 2 was from Detroit, and they promised to bring me to Detroit to be on their radio station.

The Leukemia Ball was held in a huge auditorium with 1000 people in attendance. It was black tie, and everyone was elegantly dressed. I took pictures and shook hands all night long. My job was to mix and mingle, a skill I have polished my entire life. The evening was a great success!

The Inauguration

I don't recall many details from the actual Inauguration. We were spectators from a distance, actually from the top of a hill near the Capitol. It was very much like everything else in Washington, D.C. You are either "up" or "down," "in" or "out."

One of the most memorable parts of that morning was meeting people from all over the United States who had gathered there just to feel a part of the event. Two of my favorites were retired librarians who had worked for the Ronald Reagan White House. They answered the letters Reagan received.

Reagan was a close communicator in both his personal and professional life. I recall meeting classmates of his from high school in Illinois who had retired to Florida. They had a scrapbook with all of the cards and letters and invitations they had received from Reagan over the course of their lifetime. Reagan never forgot his roots or his friends.

The Inaugural Ball

Our tickets to the Inaugural Ball were for the Pension Building which was undergoing renovation. We were supposed to enter by the back door, and Security searched us. Quite unexpectedly, we were greeted by the personal assistant to George Bush, a young man in his 20's. We know now that this was one of Jack's arrangements. We were escorted up to the top floor of the Pension Building where you could only look down at the festivities, and it was obvious they wanted to keep us there. But I escaped!

We began talking to two medical doctors from Chile.

I said to them, "You are hereby appointed as my KGB."

They said, "It's a deal!"

We managed to slip away to the elevator and to go down to the main floor. We crashed the party. Well, that's not exactly true, because we did have tickets. But when you're supposed to be "kept under wraps," and you escape, you become a party crasher. For four hours, I did nothing but take pictures with Senators and Representatives who wanted to tell lies back home. A few of them sent us copies of the pictures later.

The media covered me as well, and I was on the morning news with four networks. Adrian complained that she didn't get one drink or one morsel of food, or one dance, and that she, like Jack, was getting sick of all of the attention people were giving me.

I said, "A star is born."

Her disposition improved when we arrived at an Italian restaurant at 2:00 a.m. to have dinner. I went back into the kitchen, kissed the mother of the owner, shook hands with all of the cooks, and ended up getting us a free dinner.

Guayule

Jack Stovall was an Arizona resident and a friend of John McCain's. He managed to arrange for us to have an hour meeting with McCain in his office the day after the Inauguration. We had been working on an agricultural project that was good for Arizona: Guayule, a plant that grows in the desert and stores rubber in its roots.

Guayule has an interesting history. As a plant, it thrives in arid land, especially at the 50th parallel around the planet. It needs a frost once a year to jar it into storing the rubber in its roots. When it rains, also presumably once a year in this climate, it produces a crop of seeds.

Guayule produces the highest quality rubber used for airplane tires and prophylactics. As by-products it also produces oil, wax, and resin and seven chemicals that are even more valuable for industry than the rubber. Wrigley's first chewing gum was from guayule. During World War I, Rockefeller and Bernard Baruch cultivated guayule for its oil.

We were working with Hugh Anderson who had been in charge of the Japanese Internment Camp at Manzanar during World War II. Hugh had been challenged by a friend, the President of Cal Tech, to find a project for the brilliant scientists who were imprisoned there. The Japanese scientists developed a hybrid Guayule plant which yielded four times the amount of rubber, and it was used to plant 200 acres of Guayule in Salinas Valley.

After the War, Shell Oil convinced the government to destroy the plantation. The ordinary "citizen" has little idea how much the oil industry has controlled our national decision making. Oil is used to make synthetic rubber, and Shell didn't want the competition from this natural agricultural product.

Hugh had the seeds in storage in Pasadena, and he had been trying for years to get the money to do a plantation. At one time the U.S. Senate promised him $30 million, but it was never delivered. Hugh had a cantankerous personality, and he managed to make enough people so angry that the grant was withdrawn.

Our meeting with John McCain was about the possibility of growing Guayule on the Tohono O'Odham Indian Reservation near Tucson. Their reservation extends all the way from the border with Mexico to Tucson. We had met with the leaders of the tribe, and they had shown interest. Their land is mostly desert and useless for other crops. Guayule would have been able to thrive there.

We still have the written report on Guayule in our garage, packed away. Hugh is dead. We met several of the Japanese from Manzanar at his funeral. They held Hugh Anderson with high regard. I'm sure his family threw out the seeds. The problem with the project is that it requires significant capital to cultivate the crop. Then it takes four years for the plant to mature and store the rubber. That means you wait four years before a return on investment. Investors are looking for cash flow.

My interest in guayule explains why Maury Povich called me a rubber salesman. Nothing came from our meeting with John McCain, but it did keep us in Washington, D.C. a little longer. Sammy had returned to California on New Year's Eve without ever attending the Inaugural Ball. He wanted to watch football on New Year's Day with his buddies.

Having fun with Mother Russia

Gorby 2 with Pope John Paul (Gene Greytak)

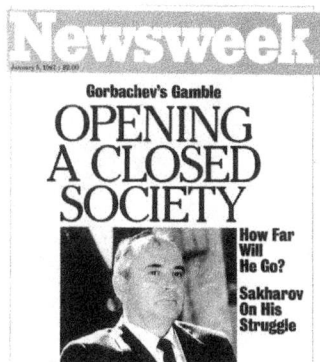

Making Comparison

Ronald Knapp (in hat), Age 10, with brothers Jim and Bob

Art-Informed

**Marilyn Monroe
and Ronald Knapp
share June 1st
Birthday**

**Bearing
Bread**

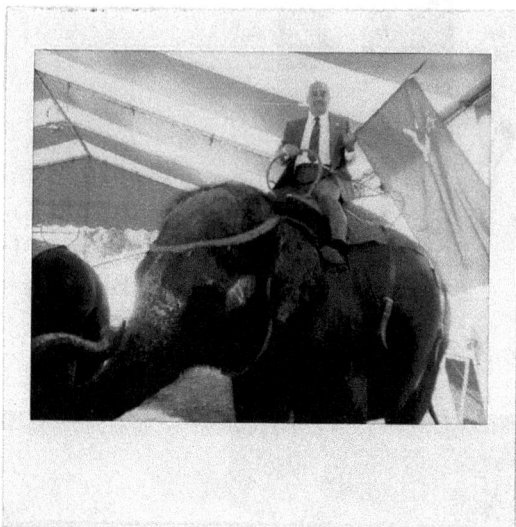

Gorby, Fresno State Fair, on His Way to the Bank

Gorby 2 with Russian Planes

Gorby 2,
Adrian and
Garrett
Moscos with
Tank in
Back Yard

Before the Iraq
Invasion

(949) 310-3698   RONALD V. KNAPP, GORBY II

Gorby 2's Business Card

Gorby 2 Trudging toward Hollywood

Gorby 2 and Mike Tyson on Rodeo Drive

Gorby 2 on Parade in New York City

Gorby 2 on Parade in New York City

Gorby 2 Greets Donald Trump

Gorby 2 at Trump Tower

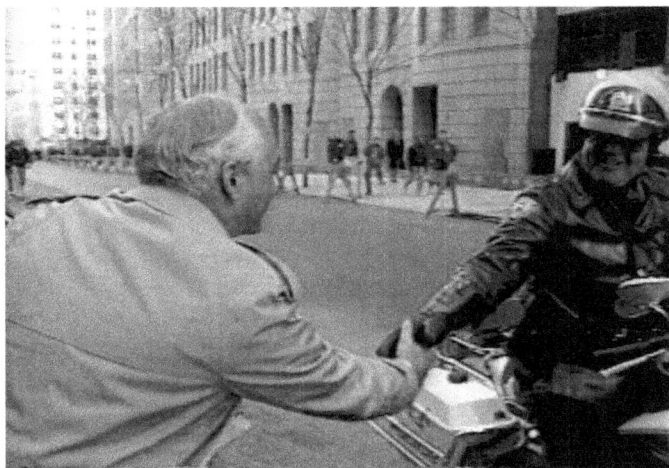

Gorby 2 and New York City Police Officer

Gorby 2 Fishing with Paul Wojtylko

FROM THE MOTOR CITY TO MEXICO — Paul Wojtylko (right) of Detroit, Mich., and his friend Ron Knapp of Huntington Beach spent eight productive days aboard the *Qualifier 105* out of Fisherman's Landing in San Diego. Pictured here with part of their catch which included Paul's

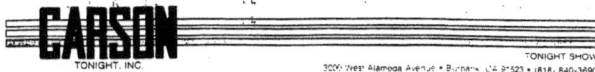

CARSON
TONIGHT. INC.

TONIGHT SHOW
3000 West Alameda Avenue • Burbank, CA 91523 • (818) 840-3690

August 8, 1989

Mr. Ronald Knapp
700 East Ocean Blvd.
Long Beach, CA 90002

Dear Mr. Knapp:

Carson Tonight, Inc. is the producer of "The 27th
Anniversary Show of The Tonight Show" which is scheduled
to air on NBC on Thursday, October 26, 1989. We have
selected your appearance on The Tonight Show for possible
inclusion in this program. Your current consent to such
use is required.

Enclosed are two (2) copies of an artist consent.
Please execute one (1) copy of the consent and return it
to me as soon as possible in the self-addressed, stamped
envelope which has been enclosed for your convenience.
The extra copy is for your records.

If you should have any questions regarding the
consent, please call John Hookstratten at (213)273-3777.

Thank you for your anticipated consent and
cooperation.

Sincerely,

HELEN SANDERS
Production Administrator

15 May 1991

Ronald V. Knapp
Adrian Windsor Corp.
14252 Culver, #205A
Irvine, California 92714

Dear Ron:

Thank you for the autographed pics of Gorby II
and for enduring our haphazard photo session at
the airshow. You were most patient and generous.

Still haven't captured a print of the shot of
you in George Bush's aircraft. When I finally do,
I'll shoot a copy to you as well as The White House
Military Staff Office. They should have some fun
with the "Boss" with that one.

Hope we can call on you in the future when we
have an event worthy of your time. Meanwhile,
don't lose your mastery of the Cyrillic alphabet
nor your finely honed verbal fluency. Comes the
revolution, your services might become critical.

Again Ron, thanks for your time and interest
in our effort at the airshow. Hope to see you
before too long.

                          Most sincerely,

                          Jay N. Hubbard
                 Brigadier General, U.S. Marine Corps
                              Retired

È STATO PRECEDUTO IN USA DA UN SUMMIT TRA SOSIA!

SI SONO CONOSCIUTI A HOLLYWOOD!

è così. A Los Angeles è avvenuto un curioso «pre-vertice». Quello tra le copie perfette

NESSUNA IRRIVERENZA...
Sopra, l'incontro-facsimile prosegue sul balcone: Gorby-Knapp, con tanto di voglia in testa (almeno questa è autentica) e la copia di Karol Wojtyła salutano felici. A Hollywood i due hanno voluto salutarsi con simpatia il vero summit che si terrà il primo dicembre a Roma.

...QUESTO È SOLO UN AUGURIO!
Il falso papa e il suo «collega» si scambiano una stretta di mano e le rispettive bandierine. Greytack, che in America è un personaggio molto popolare, grazie alla sua somiglianza con il pontefice, ha convinto Knapp ad abbandonare la sua attività di agente di cambio per lavorare in tandem ora che il disgelo russo è in Vaticano!

L'INCONTRO IN VATICANO TRA KAROL WOJTYLA E GORBY

CLAMOROSO! IL PAPA E GORBACIOV

Ma non si devono incontrare per la prima volta a Roma, il primo dicembre? in effetti

BENVENUTO, AMICO RUSSO!

Los Angeles. Sopra, il papa accoglie a braccia aperte la Rolls-Royce di Michail Gorbaciov. A sinistra, i due a colloquio. Avete letto bene il nome della città: siamo in California. Lo storico incontro tra la guida dei cattolici e il leader sovietico è stato forse diretto negli Stati Uniti?

CONFESSO L'EMOZIONE

Qui a destra, i due big al termine della «finta-udienza. Finta? Già questi non sono gli originali ma i veri hollywoodiani, le controfigure «ufficiali» di Gorby e di Giovanni Paolo II, cioè rispettivamente Ronald Knapp (59 anni) ed Eugene Greytack (61).

Il sosia di uno degli uomini politici più important

TUTTI MI CONSIDERANO UN "LEADER": ECCO

Un uomo d'affari americano, Ron Knapp, ha scoperto cinque anni fa di avere una straordinari somiglianza con il presidente sovietico - «L'unica differenza che avevo da lui, dice Knapp er la mancanza della voglia di fragola sulla testa: me ne sono procurata una finta» - «Ora siam davvero identici» - «Tutti, perfino i russi, mi trattano con deferenza perché mi scambiano per lui

di NICOLETTA SIPOS

Huntington Beach (Stati Uniti). marzo «S ono americano a non ho nemmeno una goccia di sangue russo nelle vene. eppure sembro il "gemello" segreto del presidente sovietico Mikhail Gorbaciov. Gli somiglio talmente che qualche volta, guardandomi allo specchio, io stesso resto confuso. Quando vado in giro, poi, non passo mai inosservato. La gente mi guarda a bocca aperta, mi corre incontro per stringermi la mano, mi chiede l'autografo. A volte devo perfino intervenire la polizia per difendermi dalla folla. Ormai sono diventato un big negli Stati Uniti sia nell'Unione Sovietica. Nessuno ricorda più il mio vero nome, tutti ormai mi chiamano Gorby II. Lo stesso Gorbaciov mi ha mandato un messaggio di incoraggiamento.

Chi parla è Ron Knapp, l'uomo d'affari americano che cinque anni fa ha scoperto di essere il perfetto sosia di Mikhail Gorbaciov. L'uomo vive a Huntington Beach, una cittadina sulle rive dell'Oceano Pacifico, non lontano da Los Angeles, e lascia tutti sbalorditi perché la sua somiglianza con Mikhail Gorbaciov è infatti davvero incredibile. Sembra la copia esatta: ha il suo volto, la sua stessa natura, la sua voce, il suo sorriso, si muove come lui. verrebbe da pensare che Ron Knapp sia veramente un "gemello segreto" di Gorbaciov, e che uno stano scherzo del destino il abbia separato alla nascita. Knapp, senonché sia americano, si sente perfettamente a suo agio come "copia" di Gorbaciov e si sempre parlando in russo, abbracciandoci con cordialità. A gesti, sempre parlando in russo, ci ordina di sedere e tira fuori di un armadio una bottiglia di vodka. Poi si siede, vistimente soddisfatto per il no stro operato. È nemmeno rispondere alle nostre domande.

Una qualche trucco, gnor Knapp, per render più evidente la somiglianza con Mikhail Gorbaciov?

KNAPP. «Mi credo, son così al naturale. L'unica cosa che mi manca è la voglia color fragola di Gorbaciov?

● continua a pag. 0

«SONO DIVENTATO UN DIVO» Huntington Beach (Stati Uniti), Ron Knapp, 51 anni, il sosia americano di Mikhail Gorbaciov, saluto la foll abbassando il braccio, al volante della sua vettura, un modello degli anni Cinquanta. La sua carriera di sosia di Gor è chiamato il divstare. Un minuto dopo era a tavola.

"ITALY"

i   del mondo racconta la sua divertente storia

COME VIVO CON LA FACCIA DI GORBACIO'

«ANCH'IO LAVORO PER LA "PERESTROJKA"» Huntington Beach (Stati Uniti). Ron Knapp, il sosia americano di Mikhail Gorbaciov, saluta i suoi ammiratori, alla maniera del presidente sovietico. Anche questa fotografia come quella della pagina precedente, mette in risalto la straordinaria somiglianza di Knapp con Gorbaciov. «Ho preso molto sul serio il mio ruolo di sosia del presidente sovietico e non farei mai nulla che potesse compromettere l'immagine pubblica di Gorbaciov. Anzi, anch'io, a mio modo, cerco di lavorare per la "perestroika" e per rafforzare i rapporti di amicizia tra americani e russi. Ho anche fondato una società per promuovere il turismo tra Stati Uniti e Unione Sovietica e per vendere in America prodotti russi come caviale, vini e pellicce. Il mio più grande sogno, però, resta quello di avere un colloquio privato con Gorbaciov.

Gorby 2 at American Legion, Post 291

Chapter 6
Fascination with Things Russian

Notoriety Noticed: Johnny Carson

The thaw in the Cold War created by Mikhail Gorbachev, the general popularity of Raisa and Mikhail Gorbachev in the United States and the perception of the Reagan/Gorbachev amicability evoked attention for things Russian. The Parade in New York gave me great publicity. I was the benefactor of both.

The reactions from Hollywood were mixed. Ron Smith wanted me to be among his available Celebrity Look-Alikes, but he also resented the fact that I had pulled off the parade in New York City without the help of an agent. I was also beginning to notice that the name Knapp, which is German, aroused the ire of the Jewish publicists.

One afternoon I was invited to take a tour of NBC and stopped into their news room. The staff was amazed by how much attention I received, just being in the building. They were so happy that someone suggested I should go on *The Tonight Show*. That was a great introduction and just about as good as it gets!

The Tonight Show was taped at the Burbank studio beginning at 4:00 p.m. in the afternoon. The guests the night of my first gig with Johnny made quite a prestigious line-up: Whoopi Goldberg, Danny deVito, and Yakov Smirnoff. Yakov and I were doing a skit with Johnny, and that night I became one of Johnny's "Mighty Art Players."

Johnny invited me into his dressing room as he was putting on his wig to play Ronald Reagan.

Ed McMahon said that was a first. Johnny did not invite people into his dressing room. In fact, it was Johnny's habit not to speak to anyone. He came in totally focused, in full concentration. The geniality he portrayed on the show was specifically for the show, not for the crew or the guests. Normally, he would see his guests for the first time when they sat down with him.

He made an exception for me. As he was getting his Ronald Reagan wig on, he said to me, "Go screw yourself."

And I replied, "Up yours, old man, with a wire brush."

We had a good laugh, and I adjusted his wig for him. The skit we did was featured as one of "The Best" for the 26th and 27th Anniversary Series. It gave me lines I would use over and over:

We changed the hammer and sickle to the Weed Wacker and the Black and Decker. Then we traded Soviet Generals for American Generals. We got General Popootsky, General Potosky and General Yovotsky and the Soviets got General Foods, General Mills, General Motors and General Dynamics. That was the first of my seven appearances on *The Tonight Show*.

Soviet Frenzy in San Diego

The City of San Diego was no exception to the sudden interest in the Soviet Union. In honor of their Russian Sister city, Vladivostok, they did a huge Russian Cultural Celebration in 1991 that involved bringing Russian art, ballet, opera and Faberge to the community with a series of concerts and special events.

To showcase the Festivities, a Program of the Events was to be published, and the Mayor's office decided to put Gorbachev on the cover. The person who went to the library to get a picture of Gorbachev, came back with my picture. It was printed on the cover. Mayor Maureen O'Connor was furious with me for the error, but I had actually nothing to do with it. By then I had significant press coverage, and there were many pictures of me available.

Maureen O'Connor has been in the news recently for her billion dollar gambling spree. She siphoned more than two million dollars from her late husband's Foundation. He was the creator of Jack in the Box. The lawyers are attributing her excess gambling to a brain tumor, and she walked into the court room with a cane. It is quite a fall for a woman who distinguished herself as a democratic mayor in San Diego. I mainly remember how angry she was with me!

As one of the major events during the San Diego Festival, the Soviets brought the world's largest cargo plane to Brown's Field. We decided to go down and see what would happen. I was, of course, wearing my birthmark, and Adrian had brought along a good supply of my glossy 8" x 10" pictures.

A Mexican policeman was standing at the bottom of the stairs leading up to the aircraft.

I spoke Russian to him and said, "My comrades have arrived" and started up the stairs.

Then the door of the aircraft opened, and I was standing there, ready to board.

The man who opened the door said, "Alexia, Alexia, get the Americanskis off the plane. The General Secretary is taking a tour."

I said, "Where are you from?"

He said, "From Moscow, General Secretary."

I said, "Please line up the officers and the enlisted men immediately."

He said, "I will line them up, General Secretary."

There they were, all standing at attention, 65 officers and enlisted men saluting me. I reviewed the troops, one by one. I took a pen out of an officer's pocket and gave it to another officer. About half way through, I said to my self, "Am I nuts!" This is getting deep.

The pilot said, "Gorby, you captured 65 Soviets in ten minutes. Would you like to defect?"

My response was, "In this box crate!"

Then I asked, "Can the General Secretary sit in the Pilot's seat?"

He said, "Gorby, you can sit anywhere."

So, I sat down in the pilot's chair, examining the controls. They, of course, didn't know that I had been plant manager for the Overhaul and Repair division of McDonnell Douglas.

Then he asked, "Are all of the Americanski's like you?"

I said "Niet! The other half are women."

Alexia said, "General Secretary, you have 130 kisses coming."

He walked me down the line, and I was kissing each one on both cheeks. Alexia said, "You have captured 65 Soviets!"

As I emerged from the plane, I was stormed by a crowd of people, all wanting autographs. Adrian began passing our my glossy pictures, and I signed each one, asking each person for his name so the autograph would be specifically for him.

One old man came up to me and said, "General Secretary, you Russians freed me from a concentration camp in World War II, and I have never had the opportunity to thank you."

I said, "And what is your name?"

He said, "George."

On his picture I wrote "George, we have been looking for you for 50 years, and we wondered where you went!" I signed it "Mikhail Gorbachev."

He kissed me with tears running down his cheeks.

He walked away happy, and the Russians were impressed with how I handled the situation.

The Russian pilot who was with the crew of the cargo plane asked us to join him and the officers for lunch in La Jolla. I said, "But we haven't been invited."

He said, "You are now a part of the Soviets. You come to the party with us. We insist!

I said, "Thank you. I accept."

We followed two cars of Russians out of Brown's Field. One car stopped at a liquor store, and the other one stopped at a 7/11. I later found out that Pepsi at that time was putting a $100 bill at the bottom of a few of its cans. One of the Russians had opened one of those cans of Pepsi, and it created mass purchase of Pepsi's by the visiting Russian crew as they hoped to find more $100 bills.

They all reveled in our supermarkets. They had never seen so much food in one place. They said, "They lied to us in Russia."

The host for the luncheon was an American Airlines pilot whose home was in La Jolla overlooking the ocean. The Russians were so amiable at lunch, laughing with me and just generally enjoying the exchange of jokes. At one point, I took my fist and banged on the table, shouting, "Now which one of you Russians is going to start the war!"

Everyone laughed. When people eat together, drink together, and joke together, killing each other is the farthest thing from their minds. We become aware that we all have the same human needs and desires, concerns and obligations. This was our experience again and again as we interacted with the citizens of the Soviet Union who were visiting or living in the United States.

Soviet Army Chorus

On November 3, 1989, The Soviet Army Chorus came to Los Angeles to perform at Shrine Auditorium for the first of a scheduled four -day appearance. The 175 member Soviet Red Army Chorus and Dance Ensemble had come to the United States for its first tour as the guest of the U.S. government.

We were given two free tickets to the first performance. Adrian painted on the birthmark, and we drove into Los Angeles. Shrine Auditorium is in a relatively run-down area near the USC Campus, and we knew we didn't want to park on the street. They had Reserve Parking for VIP's. So I drove up and gave my Gorby card to the Attendant.

I said, "Where does the General Secretary park?"

He started to laugh. He directed me to a parking place and then said, "Ok, just go on in. But go to the back door. We have trouble in the front."

"Trouble" was a mild word for what was happening. 1000 chanting Armenians were picketing the concert and had chained themselves to the front door. The Armenian people had been angry ever since the earthquake at the end of 1988 that had forced the hasty return of Mikhail and Raisa Gorbachev to the Soviet Union.

After the earthquake in Armenia, the Soviet government had imposed martial law. This had prompted a protest in March of 1989 at the Soviet Embassy in Washington, D.C. The protesters criticized the Soviet post-quake arrest of four leaders of the Armenian democratic movement, including two Armenian members of the Supreme Soviet.

In the ensuing months, the Soviet crack-down on the Armenian people had become more severe. The Armenians were demanding self-determination with a free election and democracy. They wanted the children orphaned by the earthquake to be returned to them.

The Soviet soldiers had killed several Armenian citizens, and the Los Angeles Armenians were intent upon publicizing their protest with the picket of the concerts and the signs they were carrying,

The first night of the concert was delayed for two hours by the protest. The LAPD was caught off-guard by the enormity of the protest, and it took them a while to move the Armenians away from the doors. The advice we were given about the back door proved to be good.

As we opened the door, we found ourselves back stage, with the performers in various stages of undress.

I shouted to them, "Put your pants on. The General Secretary is here: Gorbachev!"

They stood up and saluted me, and then began to laugh. I took a sword from a Russian soldier and said, "On Guard."

We clashed a couple of times, steel clicking. Then I whacked the sword out of his hand. He said, "I am a good Russian.

I said, "Good. Now we are comrades. Gorbachev likes everyone."

Then we all laughed together. It was the start of wonderful comradeship we shared with them.

They were fabulous performers. The concert ranged from Russian ethnic folksongs, to national anthems, to opera, and traditional Russian dances. The audience was absolutely enthusiastic about this peaceful gesture of sharing the artistic talent of the Russian people with the American people.

Because of the fast and firm friendships we formed with members of the choir, we went back every night. Every night the Armenians protested. Every night we went in the back door.

A highlight for Adrian came when one of the tenors who had an opera solo kissed her hand and then sang to her in the concert. I thought she was going to defect! But she realized that he probably had a one-bedroom apartment in Moscow, if not a studio.

Gorby said "You like him. Go ahead and defect!"

The Chorus and Dancers Ensemble had several concert engagements around Southern California and even in Las Vegas. It was so close to the end of the year that we hit upon the idea of including them in the Rose Parade. Somehow, we did get an appointment with the President of the Rose Parade Committee and two of its members.

That turned out to be a futile endeavor. We had no idea how rigid the Rose Parade rules are. We were informed that nothing is ever added to the Rose Parade on New Years' Day at the last minute. Everything, right down to the last detail, is planned out two years in advance.

I said, "Do you expect them to sit in a hotel for two years!"

It didn't matter to the Committee that they had an opportunity to share the good-will generated by this group with a national television audience just by putting the Chorus and Dancers on a float and allowing them to sing and dance. That ended our zeal for cultural exchange through the vehicle of the Rose Bowl Parade on New Years' Day.

The Chorus was grateful for our efforts and embraced us for it. My son, Jim, had accompanied us one evening to the concert. It was the first time he had observed Adrian painting the birth mark on me and the special treatment I received from both the guards at the gate and the members of the Soviet Chorus. He didn't know whether to yield to the fun or to be a bit miffed by all of the attention it brought me. To this day, he is still ambivalent.

Yonkers Raceway

The Soviet/American cultural exchange frenzy was not limited to the West Coast. It even hit the horse racing community. Adrian got a call from the PR person at Yonkers Raceway to see if we could come there for a Harness Racing Event. They were bringing the Soviet Harness Racers from the Hippodrome, and they had shipped their horses to Yonkers as well. The event was widely publicized, and they wanted Gorby 2 to do the honors at the opening ceremony.

We arrived at the Raceway in the morning when the Soviet racers were getting themselves and their horses accustomed to the track. They dressed me up in a jockey suit and had me sit in a seat and take a horse around the track. They took pictures of this. That jockey suit was so tight, I bulged right out of it. It's not as if I am built to wear a jockey suit!

The night of the event, they picked us up at the hotel. I arrived at the Raceway in a tuxedo in an open limo. They drove me in around the track very slowly, and I stood up in the bubble and waved to the crowd. When we passed the $2 betting section, a guy, probably from New Jersey, based on his accent, put his finger between his legs and yelled, "F. . . you, Gorbachev."

I was standing up in the limo, and I gave him the finger and yelled back, "F... you, too."

The whole race track roared, like a touchdown in a football game. I felt embarrassed that I did that, because I'm in a tuxedo meeting all of the dignitaries.

As I got out of the car, with a red face, I was greeted by a gentleman dressed in a tuxedo who said, "Gorby, you are famous in Russia. You are on our TV, in our newspapers, and I've always wanted to meet you."

I said, "And what is your position?"

He said, "I am the Soviet Ambassador to the United Nations."

I looked him in the eye and said, "How come I receive no reports?"

He started to laugh and said, "Gorby, I will get the reports."

This conversation was over the loudspeaker, and the whole audience roared again.

He said, "You and Raisa, please join us for dinner."

And I said, "Who is paying?"

He said, "Mr. Rooney."

And I said, "Good! We will all eat."

Then I went to shake hands with the jockeys who were all lined up, the Russians first. There were about 20 of them standing at attention. At the other end of the line, the American jockeys were standing at attention, too.

The Russian jockeys all kissed me on both cheeks. As I finished the last Russian jockey, I turned to the Americans. The first one in line was Herb Filion. As he went to extend his hand, I grabbed him in a bear hug and said, "Kiss me, you fool, I'm a Canadian."

He said, "Me, too."

I said, "Where are you from?"

He said, "Windsor."

And I said, "Me, too."

He asked, "Where were you born?"

And I said, "The Ambassador Bridge at the stop sign!"

It turned out that all of the American jockeys were French Canadians, and they all started shaking hands with me and hugging me.

After the ceremony, I went into Art Rooney's office, and he took pictures with me. And then we went on to the dinner. As we walked in, the Soviet Ambassador insisted that I sit next to him. He said, "I have some questions to ask you. Your birthmark on your head? That is not your birthmark. I would like to see your birthmark."

I said, "I wish not to show you."

He said, "I am the highest ranking Russian in the United States."

I replied, "Niet! We have no hammers and sickles on the Avenue of the Stars."

So I said, "If you want to see my birthmark, I will show you." I stood up and started to take my pants down. I was going to shine him.

He begged me, "Put your pants back on, Gorby!"

I did then show him my birthmark, which is on my left arm. It is identical to the one that Gorbachev has on his forehead, only much smaller.

The Ambassador said, "I traveled with Gorbachev for four years. Your birthmark and his are exactly the same. You are also exactly the same height."

He asked, "What are you going to do for the Soviet Union?"

I used my lines from Johnny Carson's script writers, "We're going to change the hammer and sickle to the Weed Wacker and the Black and Decker."

He asked, "Do you know any Russian?"

I said, "Yes."

He said, "Let me hear it."

I spoke my few words to him, and he said, "Actually, that's pretty good."

He asked me what I thought of Soviet foreign policy, and I said, "Bullshitski."

Everyone observing was amazed at my quick responses and the good time we were having together. He thanked me for not taking away from Gorbachev's image and said, "All of Russia thanks you and I thank you. You behave as a perfect gentleman."

The Russian jockeys did not win a single race. Both the horses and the jockeys were much larger than the French Canadian counterparts, and they didn't really have a chance. I don't know why we decided to bet on the Russians. I guess we thought they would at least allow them to win one race. The sense of comradeship was very strong at this event, and the Soviet Ambassador invited us to visit them at the Soviet Mission.

Lunch with Mickey Mantle

Not only did we have a great time at the Raceway, but also the next day we were given a special gift by Art Rooney. We were taken to lunch at Mickey Mantle's restaurant across from Central Park. We had a three hour lunch with Mickey Mantle himself. As he came through the door, I said, "You look like one of my relatives in Canada. Did you know your father?"

He was bald.

I said, "My father made love to every woman in town, and I have a whole town that looks like me."

We laughed all afternoon long. He knew Al Kaline, and I shared my experience of playing ball with him as a boy. Al lived on the next street in Lincoln Park, Michigan. I was a paperboy for the *Detroit Times*, and we played baseball at Buckingham Park.

They have closed the restaurant. We did, however, go back a few years ago when we were in New York City for a meeting at the United Nations. We went to an opera at the Lincoln Center and walked back to our hotel past Central Park. We stopped at the restaurant for a bite to eat. Mickey Mantle's son was there, and he asked if we would like to sit where I had sat and talked with his Dad.

I said, "That would be great."

He asked the people sitting in that booth if they would

mind moving and offered to give them a free meal for the favor. We reminisced with his son and felt treated like royalty.

Fund Raiser in Hawaii

We were called by Katy, the wife of the manager of the Halekulani Hotel in Hawaii. She was the Chair of an event to raise funds for the parents of children with catastrophic illness. These parents have no relief from their care-taking, and the purpose of the money was to give the parents some respite with a little vacation from their burden.

The event was a $500 a plate dinner for 400 people held at the Prince Hotel. We stayed at the Halekulani in an elegant room right on the beach. Twelve Samoans who worked on the staff of the Halekulani were assigned to be my body guards when we made our entrance into the Prince Hotel. We arrived in a limo with police escort, the lights of the police cars flashing.

The owner of a shopping center later reported on his response to our arrival. He had a new girlfriend that he was bringing to the dinner. He wanted to impress her, so he brought a bottle of Dom Perignon for them to share in the car before the event. He had several DUI's; and if he got one more, he would lose his license. When he saw the flashing lights, he thought the police were after him, and he threw the champagne out of the window.

This was truly an elegant five-course dinner. I marched in with my Samoan guards to the anthem of the Soviet Union and proceeded up to the head table. I gave a speech in Russian to greet the guests, and we shared a toast. Then I was available to take pictures.

The women were equally as elegant and as dazzlingly beautiful as the women who walk the red carpet for the Academy Awards or the Golden Globes. Katy made a great sacrifice for the event. Her husband went to a hotel managers' conference in India and rode an elephant.

While I was there, we also visited the hospital wards for the catastrophically ill children. It is heart-breaking to see the pain and suffering these families must endure. I met with parents, joked with them, attempted to lighten their burden. We went from room to room.

There is no greater gift one can have than bringing a healthy child into the world; and at the same time I was filled with compassion for these parents, I was filled with gratitude for the health of my children and grandchildren. We never know the exact hand that God will deal us.

Rude Wedding Kick-Out

In the aftermath of the publicity for the New York Parade and the Trump Incident, I was requested again and again to attend the celebrations of Soviet ex-patriots living in Los Angeles. These people were wealthy, often making their money by underhanded means. I couldn't prove it, but I sensed it was the Russian Mafia, which I'm sure is still very active.

The events would essentially all be the same. The families celebrated birthdays and anniversaries together, with meals. The hors d'oeuvres would come, one after another, rich with carbohydrates, many in pastry dough of one form or another.

The first time we experienced this, we thought the hors d'oeuvres were the whole meal, and we almost collapsed when they brought the entree. Bottles of vodka and brandy are provided every three places. One has the sense that prosperity is measured by the ability to provide a sumptuous table for your guests.

On some occasions, they dance after the dinner, and several times I have been lifted up in the air on a chair and carried around the room. It is challenging to keep your cool when you are carried around by people who have had so much vodka and brandy. On these occasions, all generations are present. The children dance, the teenagers dance, the middle age dance, and the octogenarians dance. Teen-agers do not go off by themselves, but stay and participate.

It was very common after one of these dinners for the women and men to separate. The women would go into one room, and the men would meet behind closed doors. I was never invited into the men's meeting, but rather was expected to stay with the women. This was regarded as a "business" meeting, and essentially a

Russian Mafia business meeting. The Mafia is, after all, a family engaged in business.

Normally these celebrations occur in the evening, but one Saturday afternoon, I was asked to come to Beverly Hills for a birthday party. In the early days of such events, the photographer, Don Camp, would often accompany Adrian and me and take pictures. For this party, the mother had even hired Don to do that.

Don's sister was married to the President of a major film studio, and he was well known in the entertainment circles. That was how we had met him. He enjoyed the frivolity and humor of the Gorby appearances; and had we struck it rich, we probably would have purchased some of his pictures. As it turned out, we never did get any of them. That's as close as I have come to paparazzi!

After the party, we decided to stop in at the Beverly Hills Hotel. I was still enjoying the notoriety of walking around with my birthmark on, just getting the reaction of people. We were in the elevator when it stopped on a floor to pick up another passenger. A woman with white hair, wearing a sequined dress stepped in.

Adrian said, "You look just fabulous. Your dress is so elegant."

The woman replied, "My son is getting married. I want you to come to the wedding."

Adrian said, "But we haven't been invited. We don't even know your son."

She said, "It doesn't matter, I want you to come."

Adrian said, "But we aren't dressed for a wedding."

She said, "You look just fine the way your are."

Actually, I was wearing a suit, as I always did and still do for Gorby gigs. Adrian was dressed up for the birthday party, and so was Don.

So we said, "All right, We'll come. Where is it?"

She said, "Just get off the elevator with me, and you'll see where it is."

We got off at the ballroom of the Beverly Hills Hotel. When we entered, they were checking off the names of the guests as they came through the door. We said we were guests of the groom's mother, and I spoke some Russian to them. They waved us in. We still didn't have a clue whose wedding it was.

I have been a wedding crasher all of my life. In Detroit, I used to get dressed up on the weekends and walk into the wedding receptions. I would kiss the mother of the groom, and say I was his friend. Then I would kiss the mother of the bride, and say I was her friend. I am a great dancer and know all of the ethnic dances—the polka, the schottische, and the tarantella—so I could make myself very popular by dancing with all of the women in the wedding party.

It turned out that this was the wedding of Kirk Krikorian's daughter, and it was loaded with celebrities. Zsa Zsa Gabor gave me a big kiss.

I said, "Zsa Zsa, kiss me again."

She laughed, threw her arms around me, and said, "You devil, you."

Gray Davis, the governor at the time, shook my hand and welcomed me as the General Secretary. Wayne Newton gave me a hug. I had met Wayne in Las Vegas when I was very active as the head of the Orange County American Indian Society. He remembered me.

They were serving champagne as the guests arrived, and we moved through the crowd, shaking hands with people. It didn't really matter that I wasn't the real Gorbachev. Many knew me from the times I had appeared on TV, and these were all publicity seekers of one form or another. We fit right in.

The room was set up so that the guests would be seated for dinner, and then the bride would walk down the aisle with her father to be given away in the marriage ceremony. Just as we were about to be escorted to our table, a security guard came up and took our arms.

Don Camp had been circulating, snapping pictures of all of the celebrities. The official photographer for the event was furious, and he asked to have us removed. This prompted the hosts to check to see if we were on the guest list, and of course, we weren't. The mother of the groom had already been escorted to her table and was not there to save us.

So, we were thrown out.

As we were leaving, Wayne Newton asked, "Where we are you going."

I said, "We have another party! A Russian party!"

We laughed and laughed and laughed. It was actually more fun to be thrown out than to have stayed. There is something to be said about the quality of the places that have thrown you out.

The South African Connection

I met Garrett Moscos at a car show in Anaheim. I was wearing my birthmark. As I came down the aisle, everybody was shaking hands with me. He had three cars at that car show. We started to talk.

For some reason, Garrett was very taken with the Gorby gig. Well, actually, I know why he was so responsive. He had the same drama instincts in him that I have, and he had the same *joie de vivre* in dressing up and being someone else.

Garrett had a German tank in his back yard in Villa Park that he would even take out on the freeway. It would go 55 miles an hour. He would dress up in a German uniform and drive the tank. The picture we took in his back yard in front of the tank is here in the book.

When I first met Garrett, he invited us to come over to his house. He and his wife, Jo, were very generous and very hospitable. They had large parties frequently, and Garrett liked to include us for the notoriety. He always wanted me to wear the birthmark.

He had an eight-car garage in his home, unusual for Villa Park. It housed seven very expensive cars, including a Ferrari, a Lamborghini, a Maserati, and a black Rolls Royce. I could never quite figure out how a chiropractor was able to afford cars like that, but I didn't ask.

Garrett's office was in Costa Mesa, fairly near to Hoag Hospital. One day a young prince from Saudi Arabia stopped in his office. He had just been to Hoag Hospital, and they told him he needed surgery on his knee. He wanted a second opinion. Garrett examined him and said he was quite sure he could cure his knee without surgery.

Garrett was successful, and soon the Prince was flying members of the Saudi Arabian Olympic teams over to California for Garrett to treat them. His reputation grew in Saudi Arabia, and eventually he was asked by King Fahd to build the first Chiropractic Clinic in Riyadh. When Garrett accepted, they paid him $250,000 in cash.

Garrett and Jo went to Riyadh where they were expected to live under the exacting laws for acceptable moral behavior. They told stories of how the people in the neighborhood got together to make their own "moonshine." Jo was expected to cover herself whenever she went out into public. They lived behind closed curtains.

They told of one incident when their next door neighbor, whose husband worked for the American

Foreign Service, went to a party wearing a mini-skirt. She got into the limo, and her knees were showing. The next day, officials arrived at the door and took her and her husband to the airport. Their personal belongings were packed up and shipped out after them.

Garrett and Jo knew the Saudis meant business. When Garrett first arrived in Riyadh, he was taken to a gathering which appeared to be very much like a barbecue. When he saw the hand of a man who had stolen chopped off and another man's head cut off and dumped in a basket, his attitude adjusted. Their payroll came every Friday. The cash was just piled on the desk. It was not pleasant for them to be in Riyadh, but they used it as a jumping off point to travel extensively throughout Europe and Asia.

One summer when they were back for a visit, Garrett had the idea that they would like to go to Spago's in Beverly Hills. We had been there several times before as Gorby, and Wolfgang Puck knew me. I called and made our reservation. Garrett dressed up as a Saudi Prince, in a full-length robe that he had brought back from Riyadh. I wore my birthmark.

When we arrived at Spago's in the big black Rolls Royce, the valet parking the car knew me and said, "Who you got with you, Gorby?"

I put my finger to my lips to indicate a secret: "One of King Fahd's boys."

Wolfgang Puck met us at the door with a huge frying pan and a string of weenies. He said, "Tonight, Mr.

Gorbachev, you will eat weenies! I am Lithuanian, and we don't like Russians!"

I said, "From one big weenie to another!"

The whole restaurant roared in laughter. It proved to be a night when Spago's was full of celebrities. Larry King was by the front door when we arrived. He took a picture with me as Gorby. His girlfriend kissed me on both cheeks. NBC News was there, and I asked Wolfgang if it was ok. for them to follow us around.

As we walked through the restaurant, I was greeted by Sylvester Stallone who was meeting with his lawyer. At first he sat back in his chair and said, "I won't shake hands with you, Gorby."

But then, he changed his mind, jumped up out of his chair, and said, "Ok, I'll shake your hand." The restaurant applauded as we shook hands.

Dean Martin was there, but pretty well zonked out. I believe this was close to the time when he had lost his son.

I said "Hello."

He said, "How ya doing, Gorby."

We passed a table with 12 Japanese men. They all stood up and bowed to me.

I said, "Lower, please lower." The lower they go, the more important you are!

The most fun was bumping into Ed McMahon in the back of the restaurant. He stood up and greeted me. He remembered me from *The Tonight Show*,

I said, "How is Jontavitch?"

He said, "Oh, do you mean sonofabitch?

This was about the time that Ed had married a very young woman, and Johnny had made a joke about it, saying that Ed took his wife out on Sunday afternoons for a pony ride. I actually bumped into Ed several times. Once we were both at the Black Knight in Los Angeles. Another time he pulled up in the parking lot at Albertsons in San Clemente in his Thunderbird, and we talked for half an hour.

Garrett created quite a stir in his Saudi robe. We knew everyone was staring and whispering. We had a blast. Wolfgang Puck fussed over us, and it brought us "celebrity," the kind you can only get at Spago's.

It was a truly memorable evening, one that could not be repeated. Wolfgang Puck graciously gifted us one of his famous pizzas at the beginning of our meal. This was before Wolfgang Puck leveraged himself to the shopping malls and the freezer cases in supermarkets.

Garrett was a member of the Confederate Air Force, and he had a fascination with the aircraft industry. He invited me to come with him to the El Toro Air Show with the Confederate Air Force. When I arrived at the

Marine base, the line of cars was way down the street to get in. I drove right up to the gate and said, "The General please, the General! The General Secretary has arrived."

The Guard saluted me, opened the gate, and said, "Welcome, Mr. Gorbachev."

Two police cars took me to the General, one in front and one in back. I drove all the way up the road to the stands that had been erected for the Generals and the VIP's. The Commanding General of El Toro greeted me, told me where to park, and offered me seats during the entire Air Show in the VIP section. When I found the Confederate Air Force, Garrett said, "Where did you park?"

I said, "About 50 feet from here."

He said, "How did you manage that?"

I replied, "My friend, the Commanding General, arranged it. One General to another."

The plane flown by George Walker Bush in World War II was on display at the show. The Commanding General had me take a picture sitting in it. He sent it to President Bush with the message, "I just sold your plane to the guy in the cockpit!"

The next day, I went back to the Air Show and brought Adrian. Once again we were greeted at the gate, drove to the top of the hill, and parked with the VIP's. We watched the Air Show from our fantastic seats.

The El Toro Air Base was sold to the City of Irvine. It has been tossed back and forth by the City Council which spent more than $200 million planning a "Great Park" and housing development. The original proposal for the site was to build a commercial airport. The residents of Laguna Woods, a retirement community, and the Orange County Board of Realtors ran a campaign against it because of the noise the airport would generate. The airport was defeated and the Great Park fiasco ensued.

If the airport had been approved, thousands of people would be employed now doing the construction. El Toro, as a Marine Base, had been an airport for decades. By the time the new airport would have been completed, around 2020, airplanes will be taking off vertically and the sound issue will have fairly well dissipated. This is another example of fear and self-interest defeating the greater good for the community as a whole.

When Garrett was in Saudi Arabia, on one of his trips, he had come across a single-seat airplane from World War II. King Fahd helped him solidify the purchase, and he brought it back to the States and kept it in Orange County at the airport.

He called me in late April to ask me to go out to the Chino airport for an Air Show on Mother's Day. He wanted me to wear the birthmark. I had other obligations that day and couldn't go.

I have always regretted it. Garrett passed away very unexpectedly, without any indications of prior illness, soon after that show.

Chapter 7

Detroit In My Blood

My Early Education

When I did the Mock Inaugural Ball for Leukemia, four of the men who attended came up to me. They were from radio station WXYZ in Detroit, and they asked if I would consider coming to Detroit for a Gorbachev Day. That really caught my attention.

Although I was born in Windsor, Ontario, I grew up in Detroit after my mother divorced my father and moved back home. I was five years old at the time. My father, who is another book, had beaten my mother and attempted to break her feet. My grandmother, Gertrude Callahan, learned about this and came over to Windsor from Detroit with a wrapped package she got through customs as a "gift" for her son-in-law.

It was an axe. Gertrude took the axe to the front door of our house and chopped through it. My father jumped out the kitchen window and ran. My grandmother brought three big Irish thugs with her, and she told my mother to pack up whatever she could and get into the car.

My father, meanwhile, went and got men from the town. He was meeting us at the Bridge. My mother's friend alerted my mother about the standoff at the Bridge, and we took the tunnel to Detroit. We outfoxed my old man.

My mother, my brothers Bob and Jim, and I, all lived with my grandparents, Gertrude and James J. Callahan, for several years until my mother remarried. My grandfather was Henry Ford's first worker. He dropped the "O"in front of his name and the "g" in the middle to get the job. The 'O" and the "g" indicated you were Catholic.

My mother worked on the assembly line in Willow Run, B-24's, at the Ford Motor Company. She was even "Rosie the Riveter" for one day until they found out she had been divorced. In those days, that disqualified you from most everything. In fact, my mother enrolled my brother, Bob , and me in an Irish Catholic school, St. Henry's, when we first moved to Detroit. The Priest found out my mother was divorced, and he kicked us out.

The only school that would take us was St. Andrews Benedict, a Polish/Czechoslovak/Yugoslav/Slovak school. The first day we arrived at that school, my mother said I should be in the second grade.

The Nun said, "There's no room in the second grade. We'll put them both in first grade."

I said, "Ma, I've been in Polish school for only one day, and I've lost a whole year."

Then they took me to the classroom. I said, "I don't want to be in school with all of these Pollocks."

The Nun said, "You have a big mouth. Go sit behind the piano."

I replied, "Just don't expect me to play it."

At that school I met one of my best friends for life, Eddie Moscow. I was best man in his wedding. He died with a heart attack long before I became Gorby. He would have loved it. It was a lasting friendship, with encounters over and over in the course of our lives,

In the forties, a divorced woman was in many ways exiled. To be the child of divorced parents cast a shadow for many years over my expectations for myself. When I was a Junior in High School, I become interested in the Priesthood, but since my parents had been divorced, the Jesuits rejected me. The Holy Cross Brothers of Notre Dame accepted me.

Brownstein and Brownstein

My first real job after my paper routes was at the grocery store owned by Sara and Charlie Brownstein. It was a typical grocery store with meat counter, freezer, back store room. My first job was as a box boy, filling groceries in bags at the end of the check-stand. From there, I became a checker. I also helped stock shelves, put things away, cleaned the storeroom. You name it, I did it.

I did such a good job that Sara said to me, "Are there any more boys like you at St. Patrick's?"

One day Sara was straightening the cans on the shelves, bending over. She was a big woman and wore a girdle. I took a big rubber band and shot her in the rear. She gave a great big "whoop" and turned around. George, the butcher, was at the meat counter, and Sara thought he shot her.

Sara bawled him out big time. She said, 'If you hit my private parts again, I'll fire your ass." Then she and Charlie went to lunch. The butcher knew I was the one with the rubber band, and he started chasing me around the store with a butcher knife.

I ran behind the meat counter and started cutting his meat. He was so impressed by the way I was cutting the meat, that he went to get Charlie. I had learned to do this at my Canadian grandfather's farm. He was a wholesale butcher with a slaughterhouse, and my father's profession on my birth certificate is "Butcher."

Charlie came, saw what I was doing, and said, "As of today, you are a butcher. But before you become a Union butcher, you need to learn how to weigh a chicken."

He showed me a piece of liver hanging on a string that was parked on a narrow shelf above the scale. When you put the chicken on the scale, you dropped the liver. When you picked the chicken up to wrap it, you put the liver back on the shelf. Then everything on the scale went to zero.

I went home. My grandfather was just getting out of his car. I said, "I'm a butcher."

He said, "Union wages?"

I said, "Yes."

The neighbor across the street heard this and said, "Buy this car." It was a kelly green Chrysler Imperial with a cream top.

My grandfather said, "I'll loan you the money, and you can pay me back by the week."

I did. When I drove that car to St. Patrick's the first day of pheasant season, the Priest came up to me and said, "Your father's car?"

And I said, "No, it's my car."

He asked what I did for a living. I said, "I'm a butcher."

He said, "Look at my car. It's a piece of junk."

Then he opened the trunk, and we had five guns in there. He said, "What's with the guns?"

I said, "This is the first day of Pheasant Hunting Season. It begins at ten o'clock."

He said, "What about school?"

I said, "You go to school. We're going hunting."

He said, "Will you bring me a pheasant?"

I said, "Ok, a pheasant on your plate!

He laughed.

I had a little puppy with me, a Gordon Setter. He got out of the car and began running down a furrow. Seven pheasants flew up, and I got them all in less than four minutes, one at a time.

My friend, Alex, stood by the car and watched.

He said, "I've never seen shooting like that. Do you know who you are? You're Wyatt Earp."

After that, I started wearing a string bow tie, and they called me "Wyatt Earp" until I left for the seminary in the 11th grade. No one knew where I went until 25 years later at the High School Reunion.

Sacred Heart Seminary

So I went off to a seminary of Holy Cross Brothers in Watertown, Wisconsin, Sacred Heart, under the auspices of the University of Notre Dame. It was on a farm out in the country and used as a boarding school for the sons of wealthy brewers in Milwaukee. I was amazed by how many of these young boys were never taken home for the holidays by their parents. All the beer people sent their kids there.

The seminarians were all assigned jobs, and my first task was to clean the dairy. Since my grandfather in Canada had a huge farm with a dairy and livestock business, I had experience with that. I cleaned the dairy barn so well, the Brother in charge said, "Will you do that job permanently?"

I said, "I saw a shotgun hanging on the wall. I'll do the dairy if I can hunt with that shotgun every afternoon, with shells."

He said, "It's yours."

So every afternoon that autumn, I would go out and hunt pheasants. One evening when the Brothers were at the table for dinner, the head Brother heard my gun shots and said, "Does he have to do that when we are eating?"

Brother Robert, who assigned me to the Dairy, lifted up the cover over a platter of pheasants and said, "This is the reward. He shot your pheasants."

The head Brother said, "Let him continue shooting."

My Canadian grandfather had given me a shotgun when I was seven, and I was a crack shot. I instinctively knew how to anticipate the movement of the game, to aim just in front of where they were. This expertise was to my advantage in the U.S. Army.

At the end of my Seminary year, the Brothers told me I was too worldly. Part of their analysis was based on the number of letters I received that were obviously from girls using boys' names. Also, I had hidden some money in my shoe when I first arrived, and we were to hand over all the money we had.

One day one of the boys said, "I sure would like a beer."

I said, "I've got some money. Let's go buy some."

So we walked to the local State liquor store to buy a case of beer.

The clerk said, "I'll put your beer in your car."

I said, "But we don't have a car."

The clerk said, "Are you boys from the angel factory?"

We just grinned. But he sold us the beer, and we took it out into the cornfield. We hid what we didn't drink in a pipe in the field, and went out there every Saturday to lift a couple.

One day I looked up to see one of the Brothers coming across the field straight for us. He said, "All right, boys, hand over the cigarettes."

My stupid companion said, "We don't have cigarettes. We have beer."

We had to kneel all night in repentance!

That Brother was Brother Lambert, an Austrian, actually a friend of mine. He was so fat that he couldn't bend over to tie his shoe laces. So each morning, I would tie them for him.

One Saturday after the beer incident, he said, "We're going on an outing." He took me to a local brewery, and we drank all afternoon.

I finished high school at the Sacred Heart Seminary. They thought I was brilliant because when I first got there, they told me I had to learn Latin. I had three years of Latin behind me at St. Patrick's in Detroit, but I didn't let on. They were amazed when I had mastered the whole course in Latin in a weekend.

At Sacred Heart the Postulants had to be high school graduates. The Brothers got me through high school quickly, since I came in after the 11th grade. The most important lesson I learned at Sacred Heart was to like myself. It was their belief that if you like yourself, you will like other people. If you like other people, you can be of service. This knowledge has sustained me my whole life.

While I was at the seminary, my grandfather, James J. O'Callaghan, came to visit with my mother and stepfather. I introduced him to brother Francis Fitzpatrick.

Brother Francis Fitzpatrick said, "James J. O'Callaghan."

My grandfather said, "Brother Francis Fitzpatrick."

They repeated it again and again in an ancient Irish rhythm:

"James J. O'Callaghan."

"Brother Francis Fitzpatrick."

My grandfather fit right in with all of the Irish Brothers.

Brother Francis Fitzpatrick said, "Your grandson is amazing. He can climb a tree without limbs, go as high as the sky, and trim the trees without any help. He can milk cows faster than anyone here."

James J. O'Callaghan replied "I taught him everything he knows."

About Tree Climbing

Here is a story, completely out of context, that relates to my climbing ability.

My friends urged me to include it in the book. When I had a house full of kids that I was sending to Catholic schools, I always had two or three businesses going in addition to my work at McDonnell Douglas. At one time, I had the largest Christmas Tree business in Orange County. That is a tough business, and I mastered it by sending letters in the early fall to the banks and getting contracts from them for their Christmas trees. That way, every tree I purchased wholesale was pre-sold.

I used a warehouse in Huntington Beach that had been formerly used as a glass factory. I had 100 trees ready to be flocked. The warehouse had a divider down the middle, and I wanted to get it out of the way. So, I pushed on it to move it to the side, and the floor under it collapsed.

I fell into a pit of water at least 15 feet deep which covered the whole ground floor under the warehouse. I hit the ground so hard that I thought both of my ankles were broken.

When I swam to the surface, I found myself surrounded by dead rats who were unable to escape from the water.

My stepfather was with me in the warehouse, and he heard the floor collapse. He came to the edge and saw me there, swimming among all of the rats.

I said to him, "Angelo, get the rope and tie it to the back of the truck. Throw it to me, and then drive the truck forward." I knew that he couldn't possibly pull me out of the water on his own.

Angelo followed my directions and threw me the rope. I used all of my climbing ability to hang on and get out of that hole. It required the same kind of pressure from my legs that I used at the Seminary when I climbed to the top of the trees that had no branches.

U.S. Gypsum Company

When I returned to Detroit, I went to work at the U.S. Gypsum factory. My first job was payroll clerk, so I got to know everyone in the factory when I passed out the checks. After a few weeks, I went to the President and said, "This job only takes me two days a week. I need another job."

The President said, "But you already have a job."

"I replied, "I can do that job in two days. I don't want to waste the company's money."

He was astonished and immediately promoted me. For a while, I measured the ships that came in with the alabaster rock from Port Huron. Since the Great Lakes freeze in the winter, we had to store our rock in silos. We knew the weight of the empty ship, and I was responsible to determine how much rock the ship was carrying. Each time I did a job well at U.S. Gypsum Company, I received a promotion.

The company depended on the rock for winter supply in production. The silos were huge. A crane with steam shovels deposited on land and lifted the rock to the farthest silos until they were all full. I would ride the bucket 300 feet in the air like I belonged to the sky.

One time two mechanics working on controls, Eddie and Shorty, opened the jaws of the shovel in mid air. I was hanging on for dear life as they started swinging the bucket, opening the jaws.

They said, "Look at all that shit coming out!"

I hung on so hard, the green paint came off in my hands. Both of them hid so I couldn't see who was at the controls. Later that day I got back at them. I poured diesel fuel in their air hoses and turned them both black.

While I was at the U.S. Gypsum Company, I enrolled at the University of Detroit. The company had a policy that if you took a college class and passed it with a C grade, they would reimburse half of your tuition. I signed up for a Marketing class.

The first day the professor said, "This is a senior class. How long have you been going to school.?"

I said, " It's my first class."

He said, "Do you think you can pass a class with all of these seniors."

I said, "You betcha."

The class laughed.

The Professor said, "OK. class. We vote. Does 'You betcha' stay or leave?"

They voted for me to stay.

For my final exam, I bought a big, black cigar. I went in front of the class, blew six rings of smoke, and said, "I've been smoking this cigar for forty years. There's nothing like it." Bear in mind, I was 17. The whole forum burst our laughing,

The Professor said, "You've got an A. Don't even bother to take the final exam. The art of marketing is getting their attention!"

When I went back to work, Max greeted me at the door. He said, "What did you get?"

I said, "I got an A."

He kept saying, "He got an A! He got an A!"

Max walked straight into the office of the President, Mr. Rydlund, and said, "Junior got an A."

Mr. Rydlund said, "Promote him. I want to see him."

He shook my hand and congratulated me.

I have to tell a little story on Mr., Rydlund. One Saturday, I organized a group of the guys to go ice fishing. Mr. Rydlund, the President, asked if he could come along, and I said, "Sure."

Ice fishing in Michigan is drinking. Why else would you sit on the ice hovering over a little hole with a line and a Russian tip in the water? Each one of the men brought along a bottle without telling each other.

By the end of the afternoon, they were all so drunk, and I had to get them off the ice and back to the shore. I put them on dog sleds and tied them to the sleds. Mr. Rydlund was two sheets to the wind. He said, "On you husky! Pull my ass to shore. My beautiful wife is waiting for me."

I drove all of them home. Mr. Rydlund was last. As we rang the doorbell, he turned his head and threw up all over himself. Mrs. Rydlund came to the door, saw the shape her husband was in, and said, "Not in my house are you making a mess!"

She turned on the garden hose, ice water, and shoved it inside his pants. He yelled like a Comanche on fire. She said, "Strip down to your underwear, Paul. You've had it. I can't stand her all day."

There he was shaking and freezing. She was laughing: "That will teach you to get so drunk!"

Then he threw up again and said, "Yes, dear."

I said, "Mrs. Rydlund, he's quite a President."

At U.S. Gypsum we had a baseball team called the Down River League. It included the Ford Motor Company, McCloud Steel, Great Lakes Steel, etc. We would play the Detroit Tigers' Farm Team. We were known as the beer drinking team, and we actually beat the Tigers' Farm Team. I played shortstop and played against Al Kaline when he was young, 14 or 15 years old, at Buckingham Park in Lincoln Park, Michigan.

I never made better friends than those on this team. We were a force in progress when we played ball. Kenny Walberg would hit the ball out of the park, and I would run the bases for him. Kenny carried 400 pounds on his 6'8" frame. In those days we referred to obesity as "heavy set." After each game we ended up at the bar. Kenny could drink a whole case of beer. He would tip the bottle once, and down she'd go - the whole bottle.!

I was drafted into the U.S. Army out of the U.S. Gypsum Company. It saved my life. I had planned to go on a fishing trip to an island in Canada with four other men. We had booked our air fare. I paid my share of the trip to go. This was the plan: They would fly you to the island, *unfished* in Canada, in the middle of nowhere. They would drop you off in a sea plane and come back two weeks later to get you.

When Uncle Sam's Army gave me the call, I got a refund. When I went back to Detroit on my first leave, I asked for Max, Bob, Sam and Ralph.

They said, "Didn't you know? Those men drowned on that island and never came back."

The U.S. Gypsum experience was good for me. I learned to get along with all different age groups, and I discovered that my sense of humor and daring nature would carry me a long way. I formed a bowling league, and Mr. Rydland asked to join.

I wrote a weekly Newsletter where I would draw cartoons and make jokes about the bowlers on the front page. The employees couldn't wait each week to get the Newsletter, even the ones who didn't join the bowling league. I had high series, highest score. I bowled a 279, 265, 256. They said, "We want to kill you, you little shit!"

At the annual picnic I won all of the contests—greased flagpole, greased pig, wheelbarrow contest, egg catching contest, archery, gunny sack race. I won all of those contests. Mrs. Rydlund gave me so much attention when she visited the factory, the men were jealous.

The President of the company and his family mixed with the employees. Mr. Rydland's son, Paul, played with us on the baseball team. We became friends. I was attracted to his sister, Janet. She was such a lady, always dressed in white. At the picnic, I asked her to hold my silver dollars. Each event was 25 silver dollars.

I had walked in some wet cement and left footprints several months before my going-away party for the U.S. Army. When I saw the plant superintendent enraged about the footprints and checking everyone's feet, I hid the shoes. They had tried and tried to find out who did it. The Superintendent had announced, "I'm going to fire that son of a bitch who walked on my cement."

At the going-away party for me, after the cake, I walked out putting my feet in the footprints. They all came running after me. They gave me $250 and had three black guys chase me out of the plant. They were all at least 6'6". They said, "Boss, he is running so fast we can't catch him. He's on fire!" I gave them the finger and went out waving the money.

I was amazed on a visit to the Museum of Modern Art in NYC to see a painting of River Rouge and the U.S. Gypsum Company. It brought back so many memories. This company worked all through the Great Depression of 1929. The employees built their own homes with the sheet rock "seconds" from the plant. Some were still employed from 1929 when I worked there.

Radio Station WXYZ

I boarded the plane for Detroit from John Wayne Airport in Orange County. It was right at the time that the Berlin Wall really came down. While I was on the plane, Adrian got a call from *The Tonight Show*. Jay Leno wanted me to come on his show.

His office called the pilot and said, "Turn the plane around."

The pilot said, "Not a problem!"

Then he announced "Detroit Metropolitan Airport." Everyone on the plane was laughing.

Meeting us at the airport was a Budweiser Limo, taking us to downtown Detroit. As we arrived, they had a crane set up next to two giant billboards. One said, "Welcome Mr. Gorbachev to Detroit, Michigan. Next Time You Go on Vacation, Come to Michigan." They lifted me up in the crane next to the billboard for pictures.

The other billboard said, "Come to Windsor, Ontario, Canada."

I said, "That's where I was born, in Windsor, right next to the Ambassador Bridge at the stop sign. The next thing you knew, there was an article in the *Windsor Star* newspaper that Gorbachev was born in Windsor, at the Bridge, Hotel Dux!

When I got back into the limo, I said, "Where are we off to?"

They said, "The Michigan State Fairgrounds."

The limo had the Soviet flag on the front fender, and as we approached the Fairgrounds through the security gates, the Michigan State Police saluted me.

The WXYZ spokesman said over a loud speaker, "We have the General Secretary of the Soviet Union. Yes, Sir, the Governor of the State of Michigan is right over there with the reporters. Yes, Sir, he is expecting us. Thank you so much."

As we proceeded, I noticed a big crowd on the other side of the street with picket signs protesting against the Governor. They were members of the Teamsters Union.

I said, "Let's go see the Teamsters first. My brother, Jim, was in Jimmy Hoffa Jr.'s wedding party. We know each other from way back." As I got out of the car, the Teamsters were cheering us because we went to see them first. They all wanted to shake hands with me as I spit out my Russian.

Then I spoke English to them: "Look, when I get across the street with the Governor, do this. When I raise my hand, stop shouting and give me total silence. If you do that, I'll come back and take as many pictures with you as you want."

They all agreed.

We proceeded to the Governor and his wife. They were surrounded by politicians and the press - quite a crowd!

I said to the Governor, "Who are those protesters over there?"

He said, "They're the Teamsters Union They are angry with me."

I said, "Well, Governor, would you like me to help you?"

He said, "Sure, if you can."

So I raised my hand. There was complete silence. The Teamsters were quiet as a mouse.

The Governor said, "Mr. Gorbachev, can you come to Michigan and help me? I could use a right hand man on my staff who knows people like you do. I am very impressed with you. The WXYZ people are impressed, also."

I kept my promise, went back across the street and was cheered by the picketers. They all took pictures with me.

This was not my first experience with a governor of Michigan. G. Mennen Williams, Soapy Williams, was Governor of Michigan during my U.S. Gypsum days. He always wore a polka dot bow tie; and when I went out on the town, I wore one, too. We were constantly bumping into each other at public events like the Tulip Festival in Holland, Michigan and the Cherry Festival in Traverse City, Michigan.

The Governor once commented on my polka dot tie.

I said, "Just like you, Governor. You know, we're friends for life. You are my hero."

Those were my wedding crashing days. Once at one of these weddings, Governor Williams said, "Who do you know, the bride or the groom?"

I said, "Neither, but I kiss them all."

When Eleanor Roosevelt came to Ecorse, Michigan to speak to a Women's Club, I went because I wanted to meet her.

Governor Williams said, "Do you know Eleanor?"

I said, "No, but I know her husband, Franklin." My life has always been on the edge!

The next stop for WXYZ was downtown Detroit at the Detroit Commonwealth Bank where they were having a party. WXYZ positioned me on the second floor overlooking the crowd. They were all believers. I raised both hands in greeting, and they cheered.

One of my security "guards" was my ex brother-in-law, Paul. I recruited him as "security" KGB Agent for the Detroit visit. This was his first experience as a Soviet agent with Mikhail Gorbachev. He looked at me through his dark glasses as a Russian, being such a big ham, raising my arms like I arrived on a new planet. Paul would say, "You bullshitter, you. I have to hand it to you. You fool them all! If I wasn't here, I never would have believed it."

Sometimes I get caught up in the love people have for a celebrity. They welcomed me like this all over - from New York City to Boston to Chicago to Michigan. Paul Wojtyllo, my Brother in law, looks like Jay Leno. He's Polish. I taught him how to shoot a gun, to hunt pheasants, to fish when he was just 14 years old. He was a Green Beret in the U.S. Army in Viet Nam and received the purple heart several times in service to his country. Paul even guarded his high school during the Detroit race riots as a reservist in the National Guard.

We both have a special bond with the "Detroit mentality." Now he had to put up with me as a Russian Ambassador to Michigan.

So Goes Detroit: So Goes the Nation

A true Gemini, I can change myself into the one you do not know. My kids don't even know me. They say, "Dad who do you think you are: a God damn Russian?" Out of this visit, I ended up in the *Windsor Star* and the *Toronto Star*, both asking who is this Communist among us here in Canada?

It was no other than one of their own, born in Windsor, right next to the Ambassador Bridge. It is appropriate that the bridge is named "Ambassador." The enthusiasm with which people greeted me was for Gorbachev, whom they regarded as a man bringing peace.

When I met the Soviet Ambassador to the United Nations at Yonkers Raceway, he said to me, "We, the people of Russia, want to thank you for not making fun of Gorbachev as a leader. You handle the role with dignity and respect. That's why we asked you to take Gorbachev's place at the Jacob Javitz Center after the Armenian earthquake. I know, Gorby, that you are much more complicated than people know."

The Soviet Ambassador went on to comment on the potential danger lurking around the corner, for some nut to harm me.

He concluded, "Peace be always with you, a true American. People laugh and shake your hand and want to be with you as a Russian leader. There's no script for your role."

His words ran through my mind as I was leaving Detroit, a stranger from a foreign land who received the open arms of the greatest Mo Town, Detroit, Michigan, the city I loved and experienced growing up.

As we traveled through Detroit, my hosts pointed out to me the University of Detroit I attended prior to being drafted in the U.S. Army in 1961. As my First Sergeant said: "A Canadian serving in our army! Welcome! You could have gone one mile across the border and avoided the whole draft, but here you are. Let me shake your hand and welcome you to the U.S. Army."

As I relived my past, 25 years later, I remembered the Detroit River with ships carrying cargo at the end of Woodward, the location of my first full-time job with the U.S. Gypsum Company in River Rouge, Michigan. River Rouge is an old French town used for boot legging during the 30's, an Indian trading company town.

When I was a kid, my mother took me to downtown Detroit. The wooden buildings were being torn down, dating back to the 1800's. At the end of Woodward they discovered a cemetery dating back to the 1600's and 1700's. No one knew it was there. At the time they were digging the St. Lawrence Seaway through the Detroit River to expand commerce in shipping in the Great Lakes.

When I was a boy of 12 years old, I loved to go to dumps and dig for treasure. In Ecorse, Michigan, in the midst of such a dump was a headstone that read: "Here is the place of Chief Pontiac who gathered all his tribes to lay siege to the Forts: Fort Detroit, Fort Pitt, Fort Sandusky, etc." Here was a monument to the greatest Indian chief of the Iroquois Nation in a dump next to the Detroit River.

They later turned the dump into a Park to celebrate the history of Michigan. In the park they built a Civic Center and an ice skating rink. I would take the bus from Lincoln Park to the Civic Center to ice skate, and I would skate 8 - 12 hours straight. The music would drive us to jump and to learn from other skaters, professional skaters. Soon I could do the waltz jump, put my leg behind my neck, and skate backwards at high speed.

When the Hollywood Ice Revue came to Detroit, I tried out.

I went home and said to my mother, "I made the Follies!"

She said, "You mean skating with all those women. Forget it. You'll be just like your father, screwing all those women." So there went my career in skating. I did meet Sonja Henie and the other professional U.S. skaters who were killed in a plane crash in the '50's.

I was initiated into the 9th grade at St. Patrick's in Bishop Park on the Detroit River. The Seniors and Juniors formed two lines, and the freshmen had to walk through it while they took off their belts and whacked us across the back. When the first senior laid a belt on my back, I hit him right in the face. His nose started to bleed, very embarrassing for a freshman to give a senior a bloody nose. Instead of running, I walked the line as one after the other laid on the belt. They called me a "mean little fucker." But no one in the school touched me from that date.

At the end of Bishop Park was the ship, the Edmund Fitzgerald. I could see the workers ' faces on the ship, and it gave me a bad feeling, a dark feeling like it came from the bottom of the River. I saw the ship three times as it went to Cleveland, Ohio and back. The Park was right on the River. Not long after that, the Edmund Fitzgerald went down in a storm on Lake Michigan. In my mind, I had sensed the shadow of Death on this ship every time it passed in front of me.

All of my life I have been able to project the future through either emotional response or images. I never liked the sound of a train whistle. The train whistled as my father's casket was lowered into the grave. Gorbachev's taking down the Berlin Wall came to me as an image in my sleep.

Returning to Detroit as Gorbachev brought me full circle in my experience. I have a picture of myself at the age of 10, taken with my two younger brothers, both in ordinary clothes. I am wearing a black overcoat, a white shirt, a tie and a black hat. I've always felt most comfortable dressed like that.

When I was a child, no one had ever heard of Gorbachev or the Soviet Union. The Cold War came after World

War II. Coming back to Detroit brought me full circle from my past to my present. It suggested to me that I had early on begun to role-play for the Gorbachev role.

Detroit has been devastated in the last decade. When I was growing up, the saying was: "So goes Detroit, so goes the nation." After the war we turned away from Detroit.

When W. Edwards Deming offered his methods for the management of quality to the car industry, he was rejected. Instead, he taught it to Japanese top management and engineers, and soon our nation adopted Japanese cars and the Detroit industry dwindled.

When I was at McDonnell Douglas, I observed the aerospace industry subbing out the manufacture of parts to China to cut costs. We had 56,000 workers at the plant in Long Beach in 1980. That facility has been torn down, and now there are only 5000 left to work on the C-17.

In the 1950's, the United States was totally self-sufficient, with abundant natural resources, without dependence upon the industry and manufacturing of any other nation in the world. We gave it away. Let us pray that we will have the wisdom to take it back. My experience as Gorby 2 has made me aware of our global perspective, but within it self-reliance should be foremost for us as a nation and as a people.

My Iroquois Heritage

When I was 12 and thinking about Chief Pontiac, I did not know about my Indian heritage. I still remember the day when my grandmother, Rose Knapp, was visiting me in Huntington Beach, California, after my grandfather's death.

She said, "I have something terrible to tell you."

I said, "What's so terrible, Mimie? (grandmother in French Canadian).

She said, "You are an Indian." She cried and said, "I hated to tell you."

She was surprised that I wasn't sad.

I kissed her on the forehead and said, "Never did like those God damn cowboys."

We hugged and danced in a circle.

She said, "That's a load off my back. Before I die, I wanted you to know your history."

So I told my Brother, Bob, and he took it seriously. In Robert John's search for his past, he met an Indian judge in Los Angeles who was from Canada, Judge Gabori. He asked Bob where he was from in Canada.

Bob said, "Outside of Windsor."

The judge said, "Me, too," and asked which road.

Bob said, "The 8th Concession."

The Judge said, "Me, too. I was adopted by Sam Knapp." The Judge was an Indian also.

Sam Knapp was the brother of my grandfather, John Knapp, who lived outside of McGregor. Sam was an auctioneer, got into trouble, and spent some time in jail. That was bad news in those days.

We traveled a straight line to our Indian heritage. My Indian grandmother told me how her mother died at 47 years old. They dragged her behind a horse across the frozen ground in the winter and buried her on sticks up in the air. As my grandmother walked to school, she had to pass by her mother being eaten by crows, a scene of true nature, returning to Mother Earth one piece at a time.

The Judge put our paper work in order with the Bureau of Indian Affairs. Here my brothers and I are starting our second life knowing who we really are: People of the Earth. My grandmother told me we are Seneca, part of the Seven Nations of the Iroquois led by Pontiac. My grandmother's maiden name was Soligmy and also Gaza. She was almost six feet tall, and her father was seven feet tall. The Soligmy family were farmers, and they owned sections of land. Brothers and sisters from two families inter-married. A family of 14 married into a family of 16. Four brothers married four sisters. When I was a child, I was related to everybody.

As you cross the Ambassador Bridge to Canada from Detroit, the first road toward Amherstburg is Knapp Road. The Islands, Knapp Islands, are on the Detroit River. Across the River was Ft. Wayne, the old Fort Detroit, a French fort. On the Canadian side was Fort Maldon, a British fort, all this history teaching me in one fashion or another. Knapp is a German name. I don't know John Knapp's genealogy. Both of my grandparents spoke French; and until I was told of my Indian heritage, I just considered them both French Canadians.

Chapter 8

The U.S. Army

People so frequently ask me whether I was afraid doing my parade in New York City. Or they ask me how I had the courage to be such a risk taker. I know that all of the experience we have in a lifetime is mobilized by events that occur. Whether we take the chance and move forward or whether we hold back out of fear is determined in large part by our past responses.

When I got my invitation from Uncle Sam, I had two choices. Since I was born in Canada to a Canadian father and American mother, I had dual citizenship. It would have been perfectly legal for me to cross the Ambassador Bridge into Canada and avoid the Draft. It didn't even cross my mind.

On the first day, when the Drill Sergeant looked at my paper work, he said, "What are you doing in this man's army?"

I said, "I'm serving my country."

To serve your country from Detroit had a unique character. The Serge lined us all up and said, "I am passing down this box, and I want you to put all arms in it - guns, knives, hand grenades, anything you are carrying."

The box went down the line and filled up with handguns and knives - you name it, they had it.

The Serge lifted up the box and said once again, "When the box comes by, put any arms in your possession into the box."

The basket went down the line a second time, and it filled up again.

The Serge said, once again, "Put all of your arms and ammunition into the box. If we find any concealed weapons on you, Mo town, you will be court martialed and sent to prison. This is your last chance."

He passed the box down the line the third time, and again it filled up: guns, knives, ice picks, brass knuckles, and a tire iron. I couldn't believe it.

These fellows from Detroit were rough riders accustomed to fighting in the street riots. The Serge had his work cut out for him. He made one of the biggest black guys the Sergeant of the Barracks. By the time our train got to St. Louis, he had jumped off the train and disappeared.

We were on our way to Fort Leonard Wood, in mid-winter, especially selected for our basic training because we were being prepared for Korea which has extreme temperatures, in winter double digits below zero. Fort Leonard Wood, Missouri was not a place where you wanted to be winter or summer. You would either freeze to death or sweat to death.

My grandfather had taught me about guns on the farm. I could clean a gun blindfolded. I had also learned to shoot game on the farm in Canada, literally anything that could run or fly: pheasants, geese, ducks, rabbits, and deer. He started me out hunting when I was eight years old, and I quickly learned to shoot ahead of the trajectory, estimating the time of arrival when the bullet would connect with the game.

This proved to be an advantage in Basic Training. My favorite movie is Gary Cooper's *Sergeant York*. York is a farm boy from Tennessee who is a perfect shot. He would always wet his sights before he shot, and I liked to do that, too. The Drill Sergeant put me to work helping the other recruits learn how to clean their guns and to hit at the targets.

When I was drafted into the U.S. Army, I was an "expert" shot, so good that they wanted to make me a sniper, which I declined. In one contest, the Serge asked me to help our unit win.

I told the Serge to put me at the front. Then I selected the best shooters to join me in the hole. We took the jackets from the men. We just changed the jacket. Each jacket had a different name, so it looked like we were rotating. I got 74 out of 75 perfect shots, and our division won the competition.

It was when I finished Basic Training they asked me to be a sniper. I figured my life expectancy if I went to Viet Nam would be about 20 minutes. Instead I saw a banner advertising the position of Chaplain Assistant. I said to myself, "That's the closest to God and the farthest from the front." More about that later.

I was a smart ass and a practical joker, and I got myself into a lot of fights. I also had a "mouth." I still do. That has been essential as Gorby 2 when I need to be able to turn the conversation on a dime.

We won't go into all of my Army stories—that is a book in itself, but I will share a few of them here from Fort Leonard Wood, Fort Ord, and Fort Lewis, where I was stationed during my Military service in the U.S. Army.

Fort Leonard Wood

We used to say that Fort Leonard Wood was Little Korea located in the arm pit of Missouri. We were being prepared for Korea, and our course work was directed toward that training.

In fact, I was sitting in a class with about 200 GI's. The sergeant was teaching how to attack a hill at night, and I fell asleep. When I woke up, he was standing right over me. He kicked me in the foot to get my attention. Everyone laughed.

He said, "Soldier, come to the front of the room and teach this class."

I said, "Not a problem, Serge."

So, I went to the front of the room, picked up his pointer, and started to teach the class. He loved my attack scheme, with the enemy caught by surprise in three directions.

He said, "All right! Go back to sleep."

We had a German Lieutenant who was training us for 25 mile marches with heavy packs. We did not like each other. He came up to me where I was standing in line. He said, looking at my name, "Knapp, you step out and come with me."

I have mentioned "my mouth." For some reason, I was provoked to say to him, "We defeated you in the First World War, in the Second World War, and we'll defeat you in this one, too."

He said, "Out in front," and he made me the point man in a forced march. The men were spread out in a "V" wedge behind me, all 250 soldiers.

I asked the First Sergeant, Sergeant Pearson,

"Am I the leader?"

He said, "God damn right, you are. He just told these soldiers to walk all over you."

I told the Serge, "Serge, I need six soldiers and live ammunition."

He said, "Get the live ammunition and pick the soldiers."

I picked the meanest looking men in the company. I said to them: "We play for keeps. Do we understand each other."

They agreed.

I lined all six men up in front of the troops, and I announced, "We mean business."

I instructed the six men: "Shoot holes in those trees."

You could see it was real.

I positioned the six men, three on one side and three on the other. I gave the order: "If anyone falls out, shoot them"

The 250 soldiers heard these orders. One of them said, "Is he for real?"

The First Sergeant replied: "He's in charge. Better pay attention."

Actually, I took the six soldiers aside and told them to just shoot up in the air and on the ground but not at any of the soldiers.

This was the dead of winter. It was 30 degrees below zero. We were all carrying 60 pound packs, and this German officer marched us for 25 miles, no stopping.

I led the troops in cadence:

Your mother's in the Army now.
She ate so much she's big as a cow.
Sound off: one, two

Sound off: one, two, three.
Your left, Your left.
Your right, Your right.

We sang the whole way, taking turns. We didn't care what we sang, just so long as we sang. The songs included a lot of four-letter words too shocking to print.

Not one man fell out. The lieutenant kept us out until 7:00 p.m., well after dark, in the below zero weather. Hands and feet were frost-bitten. The men wrung the blood out of their socks because they lost the skin off from their heels and the balls of their feet. Some of the ears expanded out twice their size from frost-bite.

Part of the problem was we all had boots on that were too big. Our feet slid up and down, creating blisters. We went up hills and down hills.

The Commanding General of the Fort heard we were out there, at night, so long in such bad weather. The General met us coming in. He intended to Court Martial the Lieutenant. He told him, "You were freezing two hundred fifty men to prove a point. You are a poor example of a Lieutenant."

The German officer came to me and said, "You caused me to get a Court Martial."

I said, "You picked the wrong guy."

That was truly our most miserable experience at Fort

Leonard Wood. The only good that came from it was a couple of days off. I had the greatest respect for our Drill Sergeant, Sergeant Pearson. Sergeant Pearson said to us, "If only I had you soldiers in Korea. The outcome would have been a different story."

Sergeant Pearson always told us that it was his job to teach us how to stay alive, and that is what he did. He had been Elvis Presley's First Sergeant when he was drafted at Ft. Knox, Kentucky.

There is nothing like the American U.S. draftee. He wants to come in, do his job, and get out. Wouldn't it be an improvement if members of Congress did the same thing. They die in their chairs.

I did have one "fun" diversion when I was at Fort Leonard Wood. Mr. Rydland's son, Paul, was a student at the Missouri School of Mines in Rolla, not too far from Fort Leonard Wood. He came to the base and convinced the General to let me go with him for a weekend.

That is not supposed to happen in Basic Training, but he pulled it off. We went to a big party at his Fraternity. My apologies to the State of Missouri, but those girls were the least attractive I've ever seen assembled under one roof. We got totally drunk.

The Fraternity had been piling up beer cans for two years, and they had a huge stack that went all of the way up to the second floor. Somehow, I got ahold of a robe that was extending down from the second floor. I started to swing on it.

I kept swaying back and forth in a bigger and bigger arch until I swung right through the pile of beer cans. It was just like a strike in a bowling alley. The cans all came crashing down.

The guys in the fraternity said, "Paul, where did you get the animal? At the Fort?"

No one in that Fraternity who was there that night ever forgot me.

Fort Ord

I did respond to the posting for Chaplain Assistant and was accepted for training. Most of my unit got shipped off to Korea and Cambodia. When they called out my name and said, "Fort Ord," everyone booed. I was totally pleased. When I was ten years old, my mother and stepfather had moved to Santa Monica for a year, and I always wanted to come back.

When I got my draft notice, I asked my supervisor at U.S. Gypsum to give me a resume with recommendations. He said, "You don't need a resume in the Army. They own you."

I said, "I want a record of my experience and recommendations for all my work."

So, he prepared a resume and the managers and Mr. Rydland wrote letters for me.

The resume I carried with me helped me get this assignment: Sacred Heart, six years at the University of

Detroit, 6 years at U.S. Gypsum. The other men were indignant when my orders were announced over the speaker, but I was happy to go to the sunshine instead of Korea to freeze my ass off.

My brother, Bob, was in the Navy. He had been such a juvenile delinquent that when he turned 16 years and 364 days, my mother and stepfather, who had served on a destroyer in World War II, had taken him down to enlist him in the Navy. Out of his four-year enlistment, he spent two years in the Brig, so his behavior wasn't much improved by the military.

Bob was on leave when I preparing to go to Fort Ord. In fact, we had ended up on the same train from Chicago to the Great Lakes back to Detroit. A whole bunch of sailors were walking through the train station, and out of the window I saw one of them trip over his duffel bag. I thought, "This is the Navy! How are we going to win the war?"

As he passed the window, I realized it was my brother, Bob. He was getting on the same car.

So I moved over to an aisle seat. As he passed by, I stuck out my foot. He tripped and jumped up, wanting to fight. Then he saw me: The Navy fights the Army. We laughed and hugged each other.

He said, "Some rich guy in the next car is buying us all chicken. He used to be in the Navy. Come with us."

So, I went with the sailors and ate the chicken dinner, the only Army guy allowed.

My orders to go to Fort Ord came while Bob was still in town on leave. He said he would drive me to the airport, and he threw my duffel bag into the trunk of the car, a '49 Mercury. I said, "Bob, lock the trunk."

He said, "Don't worry. Your bag will be ok."

So on the way to the airport, going down Dixie Highway, he almost ran a stop light and slammed on the brakes.

The trunk popped open and out drops my Army duffel bag! A ten-wheeler ran over it, leaving tread marks on all of my Army uniform.

Bob offered to let me take his Navy bag, but the sailor suit had no place in the U.S. Army. I said, "I'm in the U.S. Army, Bob, not the Navy."

As soon as I got to Fort Ord, the Sergeant said, "Get on your khaki uniforms, soldiers, and line up."

I said, "But Serge. I have a problem."

He interrupted me and said, "Damn right. You don't listen, Soldier. I said, Get your khaki uniform on."

So, I put on my khaki uniform with the 10-wheeler marks all across it.

The Serge walked up and down the line of soldiers until he got to me. He stopped, and he said, "Soldier, step out."

I stepped out, and they all began to laugh.

The Sergeant said: "Face the troops. Where are you from, soldier?"

I replied, "Detroit."

The sergeant said: "This solider is from Detroit. I want you to know that they make them so tough in Detroit that this one got run over by a ten-wheel truck, and he looks better than all of you!"

When I got to my barracks, a guy had a box of papers. I said, "What's with the box?"

He said, "Tests" for all twelve weeks. Give me $20 and they're yours." So, I sold the tests for $10 each. We were the smartest Army clerks that went through Ft. Ord.

Fort Lewis

The same resume that helped me get assigned for training as a Chaplain Assistant helped me again at Fort Lewis. It turned out the Colonel Spence, who had the entire Chaplain Corp under his management, needed to replace his assistant.

He was impressed by my resume, and I got the job as Head of ACMS, Army Command Management System for the Chaplain Corps. That made me the "Head" Chaplain Assistant since all of the Chaplains reported to Colonel Spence, a Harvard Graduate and Unitarian Minister. Our offices were the same size and right next to each other.

So here I was again at "The Angel Factory." That's what the troops at the base called the Chaplain Corp. The Catholics occupied the left side of the building, under the supervision of Colonel Moore, and the protestants occupied the right side. The ACMS was in charge of all of the money for the Chaplain Corps at the Fort, all religions, budgets, government forecasts, etc.

The U. S. involvement with Viet Nam had intensified by then, and every day there were body bags coming back from Viet Nam and parents, wives, and girl friends coming to Fort Lewis to claim their loved ones. It was hushed in the news, but it was obvious to us what was happening. They all ended up at the Chaplain Headquarters.

When I went to my new office, my predecessor was just preparing to leave. The walls of the office were all covered with graphs and budgets. He started giving me the formulas on each one. I couldn't remember them. So, during my months of duty at Fort Lewis, I just changed the dates for all those charts.

My first day on the job, I met Lovell Briar, a Chaplain Assistant for the Catholics across the hall. Lovell Briar's mother was "The Gipper's" sister. You may remember in 1940, actor Pat O'Brien portrayed Notre Dame football coach, Knute Rockne, in the film *Knute Rockne: All American* in which Rockne used the phrase "win one for the Gipper" in reference to the death bed request of George Gip played by Ronald Reagan.

The Catholics were doing the wine order, and I added a zero to the 50 cases of wine they were ordering.

When it arrived, 500 cases in a big truck, Lovell said, "What should we do with it?"

I said, "Put 450 cases upstairs in back of the organ."

He was all excited. "Who's paying for it?"

I said, "We charged it to the Catholics."

He said, "What are we going to do with it?"

I said, "We're going to drink it, you fool. We've got two years to go."

During my tenure at Fort Lewis, we always had wine for every party. I made sure we had the "essentials" covered.

We had some great parties at Fort Lewis. One in particular that I remember, we invited all of the chaplains to a "Going Away" party. We wanted to put all of the religions in a pot and stir them up with wine.

We made chicken, and we salted it really well. And we made popcorn, and we salted it really well. The chaplains had a great time, playing poker and eating and drinking. The party lasted until 8:00 a.m. the next morning.

My association with "The Angel Factory" was made clear one day when I was sitting in a the theater in a class along with 600 other GI's. Captain Jackson, the instructor, told us from the front of the room that we were all descended from monkeys. I stood up and said,

"I do not agree with you. We are not descended from monkeys."

There was an uproar in the room from the GI's who agreed with me. The Captain sent a Sergeant down the aisle to remove me from the room. He was afraid I was going to start a riot. The Sergeant got scared as all 600 soldiers agreed with my statement.

The Sergeant said, "Sit down, Soldier!"

I was angry and responded, "Sit down yourself, Serge!"

They all cheered, "Sit, Serge, sit!"

That Sergeant went to my Company and reported me to my 1st Sergeant. He called the MP's to have me arrested. In the meantime, I went into Colonel Spence to tell him what had happened.

Colonel Spence called the General in charge of the Base, and the General required Captain Jackson to apologize to the whole class for giving them false information on our monkey birth. We all had to go back to the theater for the apology.

You can see that a pattern emerged in my life of speaking my mind, taking risks, standing up for myself, and turning situations that could have been bleak into occasions for having fun. The U.S. Army provided ample opportunities to reinforce these character traits.

Colonel Spence encouraged me to continue taking college courses as I had at U.S. Gypsum, and I enrolled in the University of Puget Sound. It got me out of guard duty and KP. Actually, I accumulated enough credits that I was just three semesters short of graduating when I left the Army.

When I finally completed my Bachelor's degree from California State University at Fullerton, I was working full time for Douglas Aircraft, had six children and was honored on stage as the graduate with the most responsibilities.

I learned from examples at Fort Lewis. One day Colonel Cogan, the Catholic Chaplain, asked me to come with him to meet with a young soldier who had been hospitalized for depression. We stopped at his home on the base on the way there, and Colonel Cogan picked up a straight razor.

When we went into the room with the young man, Colonel Cogan said, "I understand you want to commit suicide."

The soldier said, "Yes, Sir, I do."

So Colonel Cogan handed him the straight razor and said, "Well, go ahead and slit your throat and get it over with. I have a lot to do today. I'll give you the last rites."

The soldier looked at that razor and said, "I have changed my mind. I don't want to die."

Colonel Cogan said, "Then don't waste my time!"

I tell this story because the rate of suicide among our military personnel has reached such high percentages that we have almost as many casualties from suicide as we have from the field. The early detection of depression and the early intervention require special training for the officers in a supervisory role over these GI's.

Colonel Moore, who was head of the Catholic Chaplains, was a decisive man. I recall an incident when Father McMann, a Captain, went to an Italian restaurant in downtown Tacoma, Washington, and they poured him glass after glass of wine. By the time he went out to his car to go home, he was sleepy.

He sat in the car and fell asleep, not even trying to drive. The downtown police in Tacoma were not very friendly toward the military stationed there. They knocked on his window and arrested the Captain.

I got a call saying that Captain McMann was in jail, and would I come and get him. Colonel Moore came by my office, and I said "We have an officer in jail."

Colonel Moore said, "I'll get him released."

Colonel Moore went to the jail and got him out.

When the jailer released him, he informed Captain McMann to report to his commanding officer. Captain McMann drove his car home.

Captain McMann, who had a big Irish brogue, came into my office and said, "What kind of a mood is he in? Is he mad?"

I said, "The smoke is coming out of his nose."

He went into Colonel Moore's office, and said, "Top of the morning to you, Father."

Colonel Moore said, "Don't give me any of that 'top of the morning' bullshit."

He said, "One of two things is going to happen to you. You can be Court Martialed or you can go to South Dakota to be a priest for the Indians."

Father McMann said, "How long do I have to decide?"

Colonel Moore said, "You have ten seconds."

Father McMann didn't hesitate. He said, "I've always liked those Indians: Woo, Woo, Woo."

We all loved Father McMann, so we got together and gave him a going away party. We used the wine behind the altar. There were 75 GI's at the party. One guy dressed up like an Indian so we could get him used to it.

One of the most colorful draftees as Fort Lewis was Mick Helena from Helena, Montana. His family founded that town, and they were very wealthy. The pay for GI's was 12 cents an hour as a private first class, 24 hours a day, $3.60 a day, and Mick had an allowance of $3000 a month from his family plus a new car.

When Mick was asked to do guard duty, he called the governor of Washington to tell him if he had to do guard duty, they would cut off their lumber contracts, their trucking, and the railroad for transporting logs. The governor called the commanding general and told him not to give Mick KP or Guard Duty or anything else he didn't want to do.

Mick was very generous to all of us. In fact, he gave me his car to drive to California. He said, "I'll just get another one if you wreck it!"

I remember one night we were in a bar in Tacoma, and Mick was still drinking a beer when the bar closed at 10:00 p.m.

The waitress said, "I'm sorry, the bar is closed."

She grabbed his beer.

Mick said, "If you don't give me that beer, I'm going to buy this bar and fire your ass."

The waitress refused to give the beer back to him.

The next day, Mick went into the bar, bought it from the owner, changed the name to "Mick's Bar," and fired the waitress. After that we had free pizza and beer at Mick's.

Mick was a Chaplain Assistant with the Battle Groups in the Tank Division. This is how I happened to meet him.

He stopped in my office one day and asked if he could come in.

I said, "Sure."

He said, "Can I put my feet on your desk?"

I said, "Sure."

He said, "I hear you broke the Chief Jerk's ribs."

I said, "It was an accident."

Mick said, "There should be more accidents."

The guy Mick called "The Chief Jerk" used to come stand in the door of my office. He was Catholic, and because my Colonel was Protestant, they all thought I was Protestant.

He would point at my sign, "ACMS: Army Command Management Systems," then he would turn his backside toward me and stick it out, and then he would turn around and give me the finger.

As Head Chaplain Assistant in charge of the money for the Army Command Management System, I was in charge of all of the money for the Chaplain Corp. The "Chief Jerk" would say to me, "How come nobody knows what you do?"

I would say, "Because I'm a military secret and it's none of your business."

One day this "Chief Jerk" walked into my office without permission and got me in a headlock.

I put my hand between his legs and hoisted him up in the air and threw him across the room. He landed on a safe and broke three ribs.

He ended up in Madigan Hospital attached to McCord Air Force Base. The word spread to the Battle Groups who all hated him because he was such a prick. I was known as the Protestant Assistant who broke "The Chief Jerk's" ribs. So Mick came to find me.

Mick said, "I wouldn't want to get in a fight with you. I've heard about you Detroit boys."

Mick was a big, tough guy. He would go into the woods for six months at a time logging. He slept outside. He was one of the outstanding people I met at Fort Lewis, and we had a great time together.

I got out of the Army 90 days early because I had College acceptance. Colonel Spence retired at the same time. When my replacement came in and saw all of the graphs and charts on the wall, he gasped.

I said, "Just change the dates. Just hope they don't catch you before your enlistment is up."

Pvt. Lonnigan, tall, with red hair, was a Notre Dame Graduate.

When I left Fort Lewis, they had a going-away party for me. About 75 officers and enlisted men showed up for the party. They had a big cake for me; and just as I was cutting it, one of the guys, Larry Fronfelter, came in and said, "You've got so much stuff in your car there isn't room for the chairs." I had told him to put the new chairs from upstairs in my car.

Colonel Moore said, "Are you stealing the new chairs?"

Colonel Dennis B. Moore was no one to take lightly. He had several purple hearts and was considered for promotion to be Chief of Chaplains for the entire Military - Army, Navy, Marines, Air Force, and Coast Guard. He had decided, however, to retire to San

Francisco. Fortunately he had a great Irish sense of humor.

He said, "What are you going to do with those chairs?"

I said, "When I get to California, I have no place to sit."

Colonel Moore left the party and went to his office. I stopped by on my way out to say "Good bye."

I said, "Before I leave, I have one request."

He said, "I'll grant one request, and then I don't want to see you until eternity."

I said, "My brother, Jim, just got drafted, and he wants my job."

He said, "Where is he?"

I said, "Fort Knox, Kentucky."

The Colonel got on the phone and called the Commanding General at Fort Knox.

He said, "James A. Knapp, send him down here."

Actually, Colonel Moore sent Jim to Stuttgart in Germany as a Chaplain Assistant. Jim met a man from South Africa who was coming to the United States. He asked me to pick him up at the airport and spend the day with him. I didn't have a clue who he was.

I took him to lunch, rented a row boat, and took him out to Newport Harbor. We spent the day rowing around the Harbor, looking at the yachts and the homes. A great big yacht came by. It was John Wayne on his Goose. He saw me, waved, and he said, "How are you doing, Partner!"

I said, "Is that you, Barstow?" John Wayne came into the liquor department of the drug store where I worked all the time. I called him "Barstow" because he drank Barstow whiskey from Kentucky, and he called me "Partner."

The man from South Africa said, "You know John Wayne?"

I said, "Yes. And by the way, Don, what is your last name."

He said De Beers, and handed me his card. It said, "Donald De Beers. The finest diamonds come from De Beers."

I said, "You're more wealthy than John Wayne."

Donald De Beers was from Cape Town, South Africa, and was a Canon Lawyer for the Pope. He spoke eleven languages. And I took him out in a row boat. He said it was one of the most pleasant days he had ever spent.

He threw my daughter, Teresa, up in the air and said, "She's going to be a special person."

She is.

Post 291 Newport Beach: The American Legion

I am proud to be affiliated with the Newport Beach Post 291 American Legion. It is an amazing facility, located right on the water in Newport Beach. At one time the City wanted to move the Post and put a hotel there. We have so many retired generals and colonels at the Post, that the City could not budge us.

The Post Commander, Randy Eling, invited me in 2006 to do a Gorby evening. I put on all of my medals. The Russians love to give medals, and they passed them out every time I had an encounter with them. So when all of my medals are on, the whole suit coat is covered. We had an enthusiastic audience.

For this evening, Adrian created the context for my activities as Gorby, explaining how we happened to go to New York City and how the parade had unfolded, totally unplanned and totally serendipitously.

She played the footage of the parade in New York City from Fox TV that begins with the arrival of Mikhail and Raisa Gorbachev in New York to the tune of "Santa Claus is Coming to Town":

You better watch out.
You better not cry.
You better stay home.
I'm telling you why:
Gorbachev is coming to town.

The Fox footage also shows me in front of Fox TV on 67th Street with the street cleared and deserted for the Gorbachev motorcade. I am standing there all alone waving my red handkerchief. The motorcade sees me, stops, and backs up. It got a lot of laughs.

After the audience had seen this footage, then Adrian introduced me, and I walked in from the back of the room to the music of the Soviet anthem, carrying the hammer and sickle flag, and wearing all of my medals. I delivered the Volkswagen ad, told my Johnny Carson jokes, and then showed the video "Rock the Wall."

It was a great opportunity for me to synthesize these events and to present them in a showcase. The audience couldn't have been more receptive. We were grateful to Kevin Roberts who came and recorded the evening. I have used his video over and over.

Each time I return to the American Legion, I feel honored to have served in the U.S. Army. The members of Post 291 are such fine people, always polite and congenial, with every branch of the Service represented and treated with total respect. We all make jokes, but in the spirit of the comradeship that can only be shared by a group of people who have signed off to give their lives for their country.

The ultimate togetherness emerges when we have major events and the song for each branch of service is played. When it's Anchors Away, the Navy stands up. When the Caissons Roll, the Army stands up. When it's the

Wild Blue Yonder, the Air Force stands up. When it's The Halls of Montezuma, the Marines stand up. When it's through Surf and Storm and Howling Gale, the Coast Guard stands up.

Chapter 9

Gorby 2 in Los Angeles
and Beyond

My Rapport with the Russians

Throughout my experience as Gorby 2, I have had an amazing rapport with Russian people who have immigrated to this country. I truly believe it goes back to my experience at St. Henry's in the first grade when the Irish priest wouldn't let me stay in his school because my parents were divorced.

The students at St. Andrews Benedict, which took me in, were all from "Eastern Block" families: Hungary, Poland, Yugoslavia, and Czechoslovakia. I learned how they think, how they approach problems, how they view the world. For the most part, it's dark, and humor is essential to break through the cloud that hangs over them.

These people hated the Russians. Their parents came from the old country, where they lived pre-World War II, and they had stories they shared with their kids. They were from countries that had been run over by the

Germans and the Russians, losing everything - homes, relatives.

Many couldn't speak English, and only their children in school with me were learning the English language. History from the homeland was in their blood. I was affected by their stories of misery. But in temperament, they were very much like the Russians.

My first friend at St. Andrews was Eddie Moscow, and he remained my friend until his death from a heart attack. Eddie was Fire Chief of the Dearborn, Michigan Fire Department. He smoked Marlboros! I was the best man at his wedding. Eddie walked to school with me in the second grade. His voice was even then as deep as a 50-year old. He swore like a drunken sailor, with a vocabulary of four-letter words that wouldn't quit.

When we walked down the street together, he ran fifty feet ahead of me, like a deer. In the winter he would walk with his sister, Helen. Instead of walking, I would grab onto the back of someone's car and ride the bumper to school. Eddie would give me the finger as I rode by, and I would give him the finger back.

We were together through grade school, and then I went to St. Patrick's for high school. Eddie went to Mt. Carmel in Wyandotte, a Polish School. When St. Patrick's Green team played Mt. Carmel's Red team, it was the biggest game in the year. I crossed the field before the game to tell Eddie that Mt. Carmel's team was going to lose.

I said, "We're going to kick your ass, so get used to it."

They all booed me. When I came back to the "Green" side, the coach wanted to know what I told them to rile them up so much!

Mt. Carmel lost the game.

Eddie came to interview for a job at U.S. Gypsum when I was working there. I got to conduct the interview, and I organized it so that I was sitting with my back to him, asking questions. On each side of me I put the biggest men in the factory: Kenny Walberg, 6'8"and Russ Larsen 7'2". Add boots and a hard hat. Eddie was scared shit-less!

I said, "Eddie, do you ever swear?

He said, "No, Sir, I never take God's name in vain."

Then I asked him if he ever lied. I said, "It is against company policy to lie, so you must realize that if we catch you with a lie, you will be thrown out. Please take these interview questions seriously."

He said, "No, Sir, I always tell the truth."

I asked, "Do you have any friends?"

He said, "I have a lot of friends."

I said, "Do your parents love you?"

He said, "Yes, Sir, and my sister, too."

I asked, "Are you a Russian, with a name like Moscow?"

"No," he said, "I'm Czechoslovakian."

I asked, "Do you pray on your his hands and knees every night."

He said, "Oh, yes, Sir."

I asked, "Are you a good football player?"

He said, "Yes."

So I said, "Then why can't you beat St. Patrick's?"

And then I turned around.

He said, "Oh, shit, I got the job. You sure hang out with some big Mother F......"

Eddie taught me how to speak with the Russians!

The Russian immigrants lived together in North Hollywood in the same apartment complex, almost like a commune. We were introduced to a very fine Jewish artist, Zenovy Shersher. He and his wife had the idea of starting a Club in Hollywood where they would display his works, and they invited us to the grand opening.

They had food and drinks all prepared, and no one, absolutely no one, except Gorby and Adrian showed up. That was the beginning of our friendship with them.

They invited us to their home, and we came to know their two sons. The apartment complex was all Russian Jews, speaking the same language. It reminded me of the ethnic neighborhoods in New York, Chicago, and

Detroit. They all settled together.

Our friendship with Zenovy's family led to a very awkward incident. We had also been introduced to an opera singer who had been very famous in the Soviet Union and who was so beautiful she had been regarded as the Elizabeth Taylor of Russia - or so we were told by her and her husband.

They had a son in Los Angeles who was obviously Russian Mafia, offering us arms, subs, and missiles he had for sale. We got the feeling that all of Russia was for sale.

I would laugh and say, "For whom, Castro! He's old. Whom do we shoot? Sorry, I'm not in that business."

We had been invited for dinner at the apartment of the opera singer. It was our first time there, and we parked in the parking lot under the building. We stayed quite late; and when we went down to our car, we found that the garage was locked for the night. So we went back up, knocked on the door, and asked if we could spend the night on the floor of their apartment. It made us friends.

We wanted to return the hospitality of our Russian acquaintances, so we invited them for a barbecue on the 4th of July. What we didn't know, was the class warfare between these people. The opera singer and her husband wanted nothing to do with these Russian Jews. So our big idea of entertaining our Russian friends together turned into a disaster.

To make matters worse, we were cooking chicken over an open fire. Adrian had pre-cooked it, but not long enough, and the chicken was raw in the middle. There is nothing worse than raw chicken! The only thing that saved the afternoon was the corn on the cob, We roasted it in the fire, and our guests ate three dozen ears of corn. They had never had it before.

As I mentioned earlier, I was frequently asked to appear for a birthday or an anniversary at the home of a Russian immigrant. One such party was the 50th wedding anniversary of a World War II veteran. He only had one arm. The other was shot off by the Germans in Stalingrad. He dressed up in a Russian uniform.

The room in the hotel was full, with about 300 people. His wife changed her clothes eight times during the evening. She was so grateful to have new clothes, and I assumed it was her way of demonstrating her prosperity. The Russian soldier took my arm, and we goose-stepped around the ball room while all of the guests clapped and stomped their feet. I took pictures with all of the guests for their scrap books.

The Russians all just seemed to like being with me, whether they were just talking and laughing with me or putting me in a chair, lifting me up over their heads and dancing around the room in Russian military fashion. I am not much of a drinker, but the Russians are heavy drinkers. They never seemed to notice when I stopped.

Under Surveillance

As an "impostor," I gave Gorbachev a tremendous amount of free publicity. Because I did not do the parade in New York City with an agent, no one had hired me. It isn't surprising that our government, evidently, was suspicious about whether the Soviets had hired me. It probably began during the 18 days in New York City when I turned down the offer to join the FBI.

The invitations from Russian immigrants to visit their homes probably also caught their attention. We suspected after a while that agents had been assigned to entice us to do something illegal. We were offered an opportunity to get a loan using a fraudulent bank statement. We didn't. We were offered schemes to make money that didn't materialize by people who would appear and then disappear.

It became obvious that our phone was tapped with one incident. Adrian got a call on a Friday afternoon from a man who was organizing a Walk against Drugs. He had a half-time show to promote the Walk scheduled at the Clipper game on Sunday and wanted to know if I would come as Gorby and present a plaque to Wilt Chamberlain.

This was, of course, another freebee. Adrian asked if he would also like to have the Pope come, too. Gene Greytak, who played Pope John Paul, had frequently done gigs with me, and Adrian knew this was the kind of charitable event Gene would support. The organizer said that would be great. So Adrian called Gene, and he agreed to participate in the half-time as well.

Our arrangement was that we would park on the street, and the organizer would pick us up in a limo and drive us to the Clipper game. Instead of the limo, he came driving up in his car. He said that seven FBI agents in trench coats had arrived at the stadium.

They said, "If Gorby goes on the floor at half-time, your promotion is cancelled."

So, I said to him, "Well, the least you can do is let us watch the game and buy us a hot dog and a beer."

So that's what we did. We know from that incident that our phone was tapped. The only way they could have known about the half-time appearance was from the phone calls on Friday.

Between the agents writing the reports on us, the agents offering us phony deals, and the agents pretending to be our friends, we were pretty much like hamsters on a wheel in our business life during this period. It must have been the intent of our government either to trick us into doing something illegal or to just wear us out. Looking back, I'm not sure how we kept going, but we never stopped.

Adrian and I both have resilient spirits and physical stamina. We always felt that "Rock the Wall" and my

Gorby role were not just about us, but part of a bigger picture.

The Look-Alike Community

I always functioned quite independently from the Celebrity Look-Alike Community. I might mention, however, that I did quite a number of charity events with Gene Greytak, the Pope John Paul Look-Alike. I remember in particular an event at the American Legion in Newport Beach to honor the firefighters from 9/11 who came from New York City to California. Gene and I were both veterans and members of the American Legion.

People just loved to line up and take pictures with us. As a Catholic, however, I must admit it annoyed me that he would have people kneel down and kiss his ring. As his wife, Dottie, would say, "Kiss my Ass!" One time when we were sharing a limo on the way to the Celebrity Look-Alike Awards at the Roosevelt Hotel, some man opened the door and jumped in to catch a ride.

Dottie said, "Get your ass out of this limo."

I said, "Is that any way for the Pope's wife to talk.'"

Gene passed away a couple of years ago. Dottie had us sit with her at the table during the reception after the funeral. Adrian and I both spoke about our many experiences with Dottie and Gene and shared some of our stories. Two days later, Dottie called and said she was sorry we missed the funeral. I didn't tell her we were there. This is part of growing older.

Many of our "Look-Alike" friends are gone: Helen, who played Elizabeth Taylor; Archie Kessel, who played George Walker Bush; Gene Greytak who played the Pope. Archie left right after George Walker Bush was defeated in the election. He went to his high school reunion, had a heart attack and died on the way to the airport for his return flight. Teresa Barnwell was a great Hillary Clinton. She may well be still working.

Kathy, whose last name I never did know, ran an agency, Book A Look, in Costa Mesa for many years, out of her costume shop. Every July 4th she would charter a yacht for the Newport Beach Boat Parade and invite all of the Celebrity Look-Alikes. She actually took first prize for many years.

The last time we tried to go, she didn't arrange for us to be picked up at a location off-site. Instead, we were supposed to get on the yacht at Newport Landing on Balboa Island, and no one could find a parking spot. That was the end of the Ship of Fools.

The Robin Williams look-Alike used to have Halloween parties, and they were pretty much freak shows. The May West Look-Alike would have her boobs hanging out. There would be 5 or 6 Elizabeth Taylors, 2 or 3 Marilyn Monroe's, a couple of Queen Elizabeth's and Princess Di's, and Alan Alda from Mash.

Mikhail Gorbachev, at this writing, is still alive. He does not look like we remember him as "The Man of the Year." I have aged, but not changed as much.

The Phoenix Club

I had an amusing event at the Phoenix Club. Gorbachev was in Orange County speaking at one of those Day-Long Celebrity events held at the Honda Center. That evening he spoke at the Phoenix Club in Anaheim which has a huge German clientele. This was after Yeltsin took over , and Gorbachev was on a speaking circuit.

My friend, Dieter Himmler, son of "The Himmler" from World War II, called to tell me about it and asked us to come on down. We got there, and Dieter was surrounded with buxom German women all wearing white blouses and holding steins of beer. Dieter was in a white shirt with a black bow tie. He said they were the German Choir.

I said, "Gorby can sing in German." I went to the bartender and got his bow tie. I was wearing a white shirt. Dieter handed me the sheet music.

So I marched in with the German Choir, wearing my birth mark. Mikhail Gorbachev was seated at a round table in the middle of the room, surrounded by guards. No one could get near to him, he was so well protected. They were paying him $100,000 for a half-hour speech.

The woman standing next to me on stage looked at my music and said, in a German accent, "You're on the wrong page." She was really short, in tight curly hair.

I said, in a German accent, "Then put me on the right page!"

I lip-synched four German songs, there in that German Chorus, right in front of Mikhail. When I came off the stage, I was mobbed by people standing in line to get my autograph. I signed Gorbachev's name, like I always do. No one got the autograph of the "real" thing. You couldn't get through the guards.

When I came back out of the room where the choir left their belongings, there was Mikhail right in front of me.

He kissed me on both cheeks, and then he said, "I really need to go to the bathroom."

Mikhail Gorbachev Incarcerated

I jumped ahead with my Phoenix Club story. But to backtrack before Gorbachev left office, I had been hired to do a Volkswagen Advertisement in San Francisco. It required me to give a Russian speech, and the agent had arranged for me to have lessons in Russian. The text was written out phonetically, and I had it all memorized.

Text of the Volkswagen Ad

Phonetic:

Ta kim o brah zohm dah rah gee yee ah drooz ee-ah
Mee, fsee yah, glue bo ko veerim boodooshaya, meera,
ee blah gah po oo chee ya.

Mee, yas no pre ahd videum, vrirni a, cok da, fsee ah,
na road ee boodoo, trabo tight meist ya nah blah go
vsee ah vo cello ve a chess tvah.

Mee, nah o diem sah vnah cnal iah no voi, air ee glu
bow ko vo so trud nee chess ayo, sray dee lood e ay.
Preach law vree aim eaw, no winck vox mourzg no stay,
ee bool shink nah diesh.

Dah vi tee ah jeh vaz eoum see ah zah rookie ee bood ee
um rah bow tight meist ya. Nah blah go yea din stvah
ee ah bog u shay nah fsee ah vo cello ve a chess tvah.

Ee za sheet ee prof, caj da voh
eze nas.

Translated:

And so my friends, we all hold great hope for a future
of peace and prosperity. We can see a time when all
peoples will work together in harmony for the good
of mankind. We are on the verge of a new era of
international cooperation.

It is a time of opportunity and great anticipation. All we need to do is join hands, and work together for a united world, dedicated to the enrichment of mankind and the rights of every man.

Ad Cancelled

We were just leaving to catch the flight to San Francisco to film the ad at 7:00 a.m. in the morning when the phone rang.

The agent said, "The shoot has been cancelled. Gorbachev's been taken prisoner at his summer dacha."

This was at the very moment when the government of the Soviet Union was preparing to vote on a Constitutional amendment in the Soviet Union that would gradually institute Gorbachev's reforms. They had a recess of a few days, and Mikhail and Raisa had gone to their dacha in the Crimea for a few days. A government faction incarcerated him there.

Never go on a vacation when a critical decision is under way. I learned that at McDonnell Douglas. Time after time I observed that people would take a vacation and return to find that their job had been eliminated. They also liked to do that just before the holidays. Two days before Christmas, they would begin passing out pink slips. And then they would hire people back in March.

It was a bad decision to cancel that Volkswagen ad, because Gorbachev was not finished yet. The incarceration did, however, give me some free publicity.

A radio station called to interview me.

The man's voice said, "Gorby, you're on in twelve states. How does it feel to be incarcerated?"

Then he asked, "What is going to happen? Will Gorbachev be freed?"

I said, "Gorbachev will be freed within 24 hours."

And then my prediction came true. They enjoyed their conversation with me so much that before we knew it, the TV cameras were coming up the driveway. Please bear in mind that you do not get paid for news. My whole Gorby career has been mostly news. And the rest, for the most part, has been charitable contributions. Alas, I never made real money from the Look-Alike business, but I sure did have fun!

Lest you think I downplay the income, here are some of the things I turned down. Yakov Smirnoff's assistant called right after Gorbachev was incarcerated. Yakov wanted me to come to a party at his house wearing a sign that said, "I Work for Food." He offered me $200, and I declined.

HBO offered me $200 to do a skit with Gorbachev sitting on a toilet. I declined. Japanese TV offered me $500 to stick Gorbachev's head in a toilet. I declined.

One thing I walked away from was probably a stupid mistake. I auditioned for *The Naked Gun* and got the part. When they sent me the script, I thought the rubbing off the birthmark denigrated Gorbachev, and I refused the part. It paid $1000. In retrospect, I should not have turned down Paramount. I took my Gorby *persona* too seriously that time. Who knows what might have happened if I had played that role.

Boxing Incidents

This publicity during Gorbachev's incarceration attracted the attention of a French TV group who was doing a series of short vignettes for broadcast in France. They wanted to come and follow me for a day. They started at our house in Fullerton and then took me to Beverly Hills The high point of that excursion was an encounter on Rodeo Drive with Mike Tyson.

French TV said, "Here comes Mike Tyson."

I walked up to Mike Tyson and said, "Put your dukes up."

He said, "Gorby, Gorby is that you? You're the guy who got Trump! You're my hero!"

Trump was Tyson's sponsor for the Holyfield fight that he lost.

Tyson said, "Gorby, where are you from?"

I said, "Detroit."

Then he said, "I'm about to get my ass kicked."

I took my right knee and put it between his legs in his groin. As he went down to protect his private parts, I caught him with a left and a right.

He stopped me and said, "Gorby, you're making me look bad."

Then he got me in a headlock and kissed me on top of the head.

My grandfather, James J. O'Callahan, taught me how to box.

He used to say to me, "Shake the hand that shook hands with John L. Sullivan, the greatest fighter of them all, *and* Joe Lewis. I haven't washed my hands yet."

Then he would say, "When you, Ronald Knapp, shake hands with James Callahan, you shake the hand that shook the hand of John L. Sullivan and Joe Lewis."

Joe Lewis used to come to my Canadian Grandfather's farm to buy turkeys. One time when he came, Tom Thumb and Lone Eagle, midget wrestlers were with him. They became famous when black and white TV first came out.

Somebody said in the barn, "The little guy can take the big guy."

The big guy was a farmer in bib overalls, and the little guy was the wrestler, Tom Thumb.

Tom Thumb said to the farmer, "Lean over, I want to tell you something."

The farmer leaned over and Tom butted him on the head and knocked him out. I was just a little kid when that happened, and I laughed and laughed.

Years later, when Joe Lewis was at Caesar's Palace in Las Vegas, I shared the story with him, and he remembered me as the little kid laughing in the barn. We talked for three hours. I had watched all of his famous fights with my grandfather. We talked about his experience in the army in the Second World War. We talked about how he lost all of his money to his managers.

Joe Lewis was a true gentleman boxer, a gentleman's gentleman. I measured my hand against his. He had huge hands.

He said, "When I die, if you have any problems with my people, call me upstairs, and I'll come down and take care of them."

Joe got us comped at Caesar's Palace as Gorby. We had a room with a Jacuzzi, and we were invited to lunch with the President of Caesar's Palace.

But back to French TV. They did broadcast my day with them on French TV. We have a tape of all of the stories they did. The only one I remember, except for mine, of course, is about a purple lady who lived in a purple house landscaped with purple flowers. She drove a purple car, had her hair dyed purple, only wore purple clothes, and only ate purple food.

Speaking of Joe Lewis reminds me of one of my schemes to make money when I was raising my five kids. Lion Country Safari in Orange County had a famous lion, Frasier. He had more than 150 cubs. Every time he had another cub, they would put his picture in the paper with his red tongue hanging out. He was the "stud" of

Orange County. They called him "Frasier the Sensuous Lion."

I went and got the rights to Frasier's picture with the agreement that whatever money I made, I would give back ten percent for the preservation of lions. So I went down to Western Badge and Trophy and ordered 50,000 buttons the size of the circumference of a tennis ball. On top it said "Frasier Forever" and under the picture it said "Frasier the Lion." The picture was of Frasier with his red tongue hanging out.

I pre-sold the badges to Knott's Berry Farm and Disneyland. Western Badge gave me 500 buttons to start, and I took the 500 buttons to work at Douglas Aircraft and sold them immediately for $1. My cost was $.07, so I got my capital back. In the meantime, Frasier the Lion died and was in the headlines of the newspaper. So there I was, stuck with 50,000 buttons to pick up.

I went down to Western Badge with my paper work to pick up the badges. The clerk brought the badges out, and showed me one of them. I was ready to pay for them, and then I looked closely and observed that that had a "z" instead of an "s" in Frasier. They had misspelled it "Frazier" 50,000 times instead of "Frasier."

I told them they had ruined my business. The owner came out and said, "I'll just give you the badges and call it even." He did not know that Frasier the lion had died, and it really would not have mattered. The paperwork with the order had the right spelling.

How did I rescue it? Joe Frazier and Mohammed Ali were scheduled for a boxing match in Las Vegas. I contacted Frazier's promoter of the fight in Vegas. He bought the buttons from me for $.30 apiece and sold them for $1. My profit was $.23 apiece.

Here is an additional anecdote that I didn"t exactly know where to put. I was hired to be in a video with Snoop Dogg Dogg. He had assembled a group of important people at a dining table and wanted to include a couple of world figures. So, he invited Gorbachev and Pope John Paul.

Since I've never followed Snoop Dogg Dogg, I don't know whether the video ever came out or what the name of it was. Our role in the video would have been just a brief vignette. It did include lunch.

When I met Snoop Dogg Dogg, that day, he said to me, "What do you think of my music?"

I said, "Your music sucks!"

He said, "Gorby, you come sit by me at the head of the table. You're the only honest man here. You're the one who tells the truth."

Then he instructed the waiter serving the food: "You bring Gorby a whole chicken, not a half chicken. He's my man!" He put the Pope at the other end of the table.

Mexico City

Telemundo invited a whole slew of Celebrity Look-Alikes to Mexico City to do a special TV presentation. It included Elizabeth Taylor, the Pope, Queen Elizabeth, and of course, me, Mikhail Gorbachev. I don't remember the rest.

The Pope and I were the most important. When we landed at the airport, I found myself stuck with the Queen's suitcase—it was too heavy for her to carry.

We got into the taxi and headed to the El Presidente Hotel. The Pope, Gene Greytak, was met immediately and told that he could not wear the Pope's robes in Mexico City. It is a Catholic country and that was forbidden. I was given four security agents to guard me at all times, even when I was in my room at night.

It turned out that Mikhail Gorbachev arrived at the airport shortly after I did, and it created quite a stir in Mexico City. In some ways, it was similar to my experience in New York City , arriving on the same day that Gorbachev arrived to address the United Nations. Mexico City was primed for his visit, and everywhere I went, I was mobbed.

I recall going up the escalator in a shopping mall and being deluged by people wanting my autograph. They were grabbing greeting cards off the shelf to get my autograph. The agent who organized the tour was on the escalator with me, and he was terrified by the assault.

He said, "What should we do?"

I said, "Grab a pen and start signing Gorbachev's name."

I knew that Gorbachev was popular in the United States, but I had no idea how popular he was South of the Border as well.

A group of Brazilians was staying at the hotel, and they cornered me and invited me to their table. They actually wanted me to come to Brazil to advertise their products. The Pope and the agent kept circling the table, wanting to know what we were talking about. They thought that if I ended up doing any business in Mexico City, they deserved a piece of the action.

In retrospect, I should have gone to Brazil. The agent, however, would not give me my check for the job until we were on our way back. Adrian and I needed the money, so I let the Brazil opportunity go. I did fix the agent, however, when I got to the plane.

I picked up the microphone from the woman checking reservations and said, " I need to talk to the head of the airport. "

He said, "I'll be right there."

When he came, I said, "Are you going to let Mikhail Gorbachev, the Secretary General of the Soviet Union, sit in the economy class?"

He said, "Oh, no, Mr. Secretary. You are going to sit in First Class, and the menu is steak and chicken."

Then he asked, "What should we do with your friend?"

I said, "Put him in baggage!"

So, I sat in first class, drank champagne and ate filet mignon, and the agent was stuck in economy. He never got me another job! The Pope and Elizabeth Taylor stayed on in Mexico City for a few days as "tourists." Need I say more!

Trade Shows: Chicago, Anaheim, Nashville, San Antonio

One job did pay well: The Housewares Show at the McCormick Center in Chicago. My job was to attract people to the Faberware exhibit by taking pictures with people. They had a full-time photographer with me at the booth, and I took pictures eight hours a day with people and then signed them. They stood in long lines waiting to have their picture taken with Gorbachev.

I especially remember one incident when a big Polish gentleman came up to me and asked if I had autographed a picture for his wife. I thought he was going to punch me. Evidently I wrote something suggestive on her picture. As I recall, it was: "You're the most beautiful woman in the world. Dump your husband and call me!" I signed it "Gorby."

Instead of putting up his dukes to hit me, he said, "Will you take a picture with me, too? And please sign it."

It was amazing how popular Gorbachev was in Chicago. Also, I was surprised to see Robert Downey, Jr. at that show. He had been arrested again for drugs, and was on his way back to jail. His father had recently passed away, and I had known his father. We talked for about an hour, and I remember telling him it's never too late to pick your life back up. The Iron Man has certainly successfully done that!

The most fun we had in Chicago was at the Hilton Hotel. They had a pub there named Kitty O'Shea's, a welcome relief after a whole day of taking pictures and signing autographs.

When I walked through the door, I was greeted by a group of 25 Australians.

They looked at me and said, "The Yanks have done it again."

We exchanged a few barbs and laughs, and I told them: "Gorby can do the Irish Jig."

They said, "If you do the Irish Jig, we buy."

I said, "As soon as I come back from the Irish Washer Woman."

They laughed.

When I came back, I did the Jig, and the Guinness flowed freely, all night long. I had as many as nine bottle of Guinness in front of me.

We went back to the pub every night. Each time we had a great time with the Australians. This Irish pub employed interns from Ireland. Every young man was named Patrick, with red hair! They would say in their Irish brogue, "Look at the Russian doing the Jig. He's good! He's good!"

Anaheim Convention Center

A multi-level marketing group, now defunct, invited me to speak at their big meeting at the Anaheim Convention Center. I say it is now defunct because when the truth came out about it, as so often happens with multi-level marketing, the founders had misrepresented the product and the structure. It turned out this group had actually met in prison and cooked up the scheme they sold to thousands of people before it disintegrated.

I was introduced to 3000 people gathered at the Anaheim Convention Center as Mikhail Gorbachev. When I walked out on the stage, wearing the birthmark, they all stood up and cheered. I proceeded to give them the Volkswagen commercial in Russian, which I then interpreted as the jokes from Johnny Carson's scriptwriters for *The Tonight Show*.

I told them that I had agreed to trade the hammer and the sickle for the Weed Wacker and the Black and Decker. I told them I had agreed to trade Soviet generals for Americansky Generals: General Poputsky, General

Totototsky and General Kokotsky for the American generals: General Motors, General Electric, General Dynamics., and General Foods. I followed it with a brief motivational message to have faith in themselves, in their product, in their work, and in their team.

They gave me a standing ovation that lasted about five minutes. As they poured out of the Convention Center, I was mobbed with people requesting autographs and wanting to take pictures with me.

Mob reaction is fascinating. Those people didn't really care whether I was the real thing. They just wanted to feel enthusiastic and euphoric. My job was to get the adrenalin flowing, and it worked.

Nashville and San Antonio

Adrian was working for a software company that has since gone bankrupt, so it will remain nameless. We did two trade shows for them. I went as Gorby to attract people to the booth. One was in Nashville, so we had the chance to experience the Grand Ole Opry.

The highlight of that show was meeting the wife of Minnesota Fats, the legendary pool master. She was a delightful woman, full of stories about her husband. If you Google Minnesota Fats, you will find a long list of pool tables and billiard tables for sale on the internet that bear his name. It was apparent that his wife never made any money from that. She was living on the fringe of poverty when we met her.

The other trade show we did was in San Antonio, Texas. We went to the River Walk every evening. One night we walked into a bar and restaurant that featured a piano player. When he saw Gorbachev enter the room, he started playing the Cossack dance song, and I squatted down and kicked out my feet. Soon everyone was clapping in time to the music. When that was over, he began playing the music from Zorba the Greek, and soon we had the whole group dancing in line around the room.

Our hotel was just two blocks away from the River Walk. The neighborhood changes rapidly after you leave the bright lights and happy crowds and gets pretty run down and desolate. On the way back to the hotel, two black men with guns confronted us.

One of them said, "Give us your money."

I said, "What are your names?"

They said, "Why do you need our names for? We just want your money."

I had my hand inside my coat and stuck out my finger so that it looked like I could have a weapon in there.

I said, "Because, I'm going to count to three, and then I am going to shoot you both."

The one guy said, "Where are you from?"

I said, "Detroit."

He said, "Oh, shit!"

And then they both took off. Of course, I didn't have a gun, just guts.

Mission San Juan Capistrano

For many years I was active in the Parish of the Mission San Juan Capistrano. The Mission is as old as our nation, founded in 1776. The oldest building in California still in use, the Serra Chapel, was built in 1782, and is also called Father Serra's Church because it is the only building where it is documented that Padre Junipero Serra celebrated mass there.

Father Serra, a Franciscan Friar, traveled the whole coast of California on foot, founding missions as he went: San Diego, San Luis Rey, San Juan Capistrano, Los Angeles, Santa Barbara, Santa Cruz - to name only a few. The Mission San Juan Capistrano is known throughout the world for "The Return of the Swallows" traditionally celebrated on March 19th, St. Joseph's Day.

The community celebrates with a parade on St. Joseph's Day, and is said to be only non-motorized parade in the country. Everyone either walks, rides horseback, or is pulled by a horse in a wagon. The whole town shows up, many in costume, especially the "desperados" on horseback with their silver spurs and Stetson hats.

California's first vineyard was located on the Mission grounds, with the planting of the Mission or Criollo grape in 1779. Today the Mission is both an active church and a museum which demonstrates the history of the union between the padres and the local Indians in building the Mission.

In the 1800's the Mission fell on hard times and the Franciscans all but abandoned it. In 1865, however, President Abraham Lincoln signed a proclamation that restored ownership of the Mission proper to the Roman Catholic Church. Today it is a Minor Basilica and a very thriving parish.

For more than four decades the Mission flourished under the devoted leadership of Monseigneur Paul Martin. He had a magnetic personality and a humility that bound the people of the parish to him. You would find him on Easter Sunday out in the street directing traffic. He was the brother of Mary Martin of *Peter Pan* fame.

You may be wondering what all of this history has to do with my role as an "impostor." One incident occurred when the Choir from the Ukraine came to the Mission to perform. They arrived in a fleet of busses, 200 singers. I attended the concert wearing the birthmark, and I sat right in the front row. They were all giggling and pointing at me. When the concert was over, they had a stampede swarming around me to get my autograph and to take pictures with me.

That was a single incident. Another role lasted for me for eight years. The Music Director at the Mission, Ronnie Meyers, had the idea to put on a Passion Play for Good Friday. I had purchased a Caesar outfit from

Caesar's Palace in Las Vegas at the swap meet, and I stopped by the Mission during rehearsal to offer it to Ronnie as a costume. Ronnie said he wanted me to wear it and to be in the Passion Play.

That began my role as the Head Roman Soldier. The first year we did it, we did it inside the church. Adrian sewed the tunics for the Roman Soldiers that year, and it really was in the tradition of the medieval Miracle plays. My job was to nail Jesus to the cross. No one else wanted to do it. I said, "If you want someone to nail Jesus, bring him in from Detroit." That first year, I hit the board so hard that it broke and sailed right past Father Martin, who was sitting in the front row.

We did the Passion Play on Good Friday for eight years. Each year it became more elaborate and more and more people were involved. We bought costumes, and we moved it to the Mission Grounds, using the roofs of the buildings with lighting to create drama, bringing in live animals. Our last performance more than 3000 people attended, and they blocked up the streets of San Juan Capistrano standing in line to get in.

By the 8th year, the Roman Soldiers were pretty good at their sword handling. Father Martin had me come out in full Roman regalia with my sword and seven-foot spear to address the morning congregation. My job was to get their attention so they would come to the Passion Play. I drew my sword and banged my spear on the floor three times. There was total silence. Not even the babies were crying. That never happens in a Catholic Church.

I shouted, "I'm looking for Jesus Christ. Don't look at me. Look under your pews." They were all startled. I heard one lady say, "Who is that Man?" They were scared. I shouted, "Your attendance is mandatory for Good Friday on the Mission grounds." They stood in total fear.

The richest man in the parish said, "I have goose bumps. You scared the crap out of me." Father Martin said, "You did it. You got their attention."

The afternoon of the Passion Play was very hot, and the Roman Soldiers were on break from the final "dress" rehearsal. We were all wearing our tunics and gold helmets, and we had our swords. One of the soldiers said, "Let's walk down to the Swallows Inn and get a beer."

So eight of us in Roman outfits started down the streets of San Juan to the Swallows Inn where all of the desperados hang out. I said to the bartender, "Set 'em up." He poured out eight glasses of beer and was looking for someone to pay. Then one of the guys said, "We don't have any money." All of our wallets were back at the Mission. The bartender thought we were from USC - in Trojan outfits.

I said, "We don't need money. We have swords." Ronnie Muscarella said, "Gorby, you could get us in a lot of trouble." I said, "Well, Ronnie, if they come looking for someone, they'll be looking for "Ron." I said to the bartender, "The drinks are on the house." Actually, he poured us three beers. That got us primed for our roles for the evening!

Monseigneur Martin retired, and the Passion Play was discontinued. It had been a great way for the people of the Parish to get together and a wonderful community builder. Everything has a season.

Tiananmen Square in New York City

I don't remember what exact job took me to New York City, but we were there in June of 1989, exactly at the time when the demonstrations were taking place in the United States to protest the massacre of students by the Chinese government on June 3 and 4, 1989.

You may recall that Chinese students began a massive demonstration for democratic reform on Tiananmen Square in April of 1989.

The students were joined by workers, intellectuals, and civil servants, until over a million people filled the square.

Deng Xiaoping denounced the protests and answered the protesters demands that the leadership resign with the use of military suppression. On the nights of June 3 and 4, with troops and tanks, thousands were killed to quell a "counter-revolutionary rebellion" and a number of the student leaders were arrested.

The media in the United States regarded this event as a demonstration of China's violation of human rights, and they gave it tremendous publicity. We got out of a taxi to join the line to take the Staten Island Ferry. Nearby, a large group of American/Chinese with flags and banners were protesting the massacre in Tiananmen Square. I was wearing the birthmark.

Four of the Chinese students saw me, and came over to me and said, "Mr. Gorbachev, what do you think of the actions of the government against the students in Tiananmen Square?"

I said, "I think it is scandalous, and I support the Chinese students and the people of China."

They said, "Would you speak to the Chinese people."

I said, "Of course, I will."

They said, "Then come with us." They took my arms, two on each side, and marched me across the street to the protestors. When I got there, I raised by arms in a Nixon-like manner to show my support.

An elderly short, bald gentleman, probably in his 80's, was standing in the first line, I bent down and kissed him on top of his head. The crowd went wild! I stayed there with them for half an hour, shaking hands and taking pictures with all the protestors. This was on the evening news, and French TV, who was nearby, filmed it for Europe.

In the recent book, *Lee Kuan Yew: The Grand Master's Insights on China, the United States, and the World,* Graham Allison and Robert D. Blackwill synthesize interviews and statements made by Lee Kuan Yew, whose vision, decisions, values, and policy shaped modern Singapore. Yew regards the sacrifice of 200,000 students by Deng Xiaoping to quell the revolution as essential to building China into the power it has become today.

We, in the United States, continue to value our freedom, our right to protest, and our high premium that we place on human rights. It was symbolic that after my encounter with the Chinese protestors of the Tiananmen Square Massacre, we did finally get on the Ferry.

The Staten Island Ferry passes Ellis Island, where so many seeking a better life landed when they first came to America as immigrants. As it circled the Statue of Liberty, we felt the joy and pride we have to be Americans in a profound way, much intensified by our sorrow over the events that had just taken place in Communist China. May we cherish our liberty and protect the system of government that has put it in place.

Chapter 10

History Will Decide

Ronald Reagan is often cited for winning the Cold War against the Soviet Union with his famous statement: "Mr.Gorbachev, take down that wall." It was, however, Gorbachev who took that wall down.

In fact it was Gorbachev who announced Soviet plans for the "transition from the economy of armaments to an economy of disarmament" in his December 1988 speech to the United Nations, the speech he delivered before he and Raisa were called back to the Soviet Union by the earthquake in Armenia.

In that speech he announced that the Soviet Union was reducing its armed forces by 500,000 men, that they would by 1991 withdraw six tank divisions from East Germany, Czechoslovakia and Hungary reducing by 50,000 the Soviet forces stationed in those countries.

He proposed a 50 percent reduction in offensive strategic arms to the military powers in the United Nations, and he urged banning weapons in outer space. He asked the United Nations to broker a cease-fire in Afghanistan, ending the nine-year war with that country.

He requested a "joint effort to put an end to an era of wars, confrontation and regional conflicts, to aggressions against nature, to the terror of hunger and poverty as well as to political terrorism."

The New York Times called it "the greatest act of statesmanship since Wilson's Fourteen Points in 1918 or Roosevelt and Churchill's Atlantic Charter in 1941." On November 9, 1989, eleven months after his speech to the United Nations, the Berlin Wall came down.

Oliver Stone and Peter Kuznick summarize this event in *The Untold History of the United States*: "A peaceful revolution had occurred across the socialist block as citizens, burdened by decades of government repression and bureaucratic ineptitude, clamored for a better life. Gorbachev rejected the long-held view that controlling Eastern Europe was crucial to Soviet security." (469) They say of him: "The most visionary and transformative leader of the of the twentieth century had yielded power." (482)

Unfortunately, the United States did not end its participation in the era of wars. Since the fall of the Berlin Wall, we have found ourselves mired in conflict in Iraq and Afghanistan.

Gorbachev's intent for an orderly constitutional transition in the Soviet Union was crushed. He resigned on Christmas Day in 1991, replaced by the flamboyant and misguided Boris Yeltsin.

As the College of Cardinals was preparing to vote for a new Pope, on Saturday, March 9, 2013, *The Wall Street Journal's* "Review" section ran a series of articles on "What the Next Pope Should Be." James Carrol's column was entitled: "A Catholic Gorbachev."

He commented: "The new pope must do as Mr. Gorbachev did--challenge his ruling elite, lay bare his power center's secrets and sideline the bureaucracies that oppose reform. He must understand the Church will not succeed in standing against the principles of accountability, transparency , and electoral governance that have transformed human aspiration around the globe."

Isn't it amazing that many of us, who share the belief that Mikhail Gorbachev was the greatest leader of the last half of the 20th century, see him as the one who had the courage to confront a system that wasn't working and to set about dismantling it.

We have a system in Washington D.C. that is no longer working efficiently. Who will have the courage to break the bondage of special interests and confront the issues that must be changed?

I have had the opportunity to enjoy the fruit of the good will Mikhail Gorbachev generated throughout the world and the popularity he gained in the United States. How fortunate for me that I looked like him.

I hope you have enjoyed sharing the unexpected, unplanned, unanticipated, and totally spontaneous events that have unfolded in my life.

Life is a progress and a process, a journey with signposts and experiences along the way that prepare you to meet the next challenge and take command of the next encounter. Certain elements in my life were steadfast - my grandparents and my Catholic faith. For the rest, it was a question of how I would surmount the next obstacle.

This taught me to think on my feet. I am blessed with a sharp wit and a quick tongue. Half Irish, I have kissed the blarney stone. Without this, I could never have pulled off that parade in New York City that identified me as a "Great Impostor."

I pay tribute to my experience growing up in Detroit and in the U.S. Army, to the people who encouraged me along the way, and to the people who got in my way.

Think of what this freaky chance of looking like someone else has done for me. I have had so much fun, met so many people, gone so many places, and done so many things. Along the way, I have spread joy through laughter. I hope I have brightened your day! Do me a favor. The next time you confront a risk: Take it!

Afterword

Here are a few excerpts from articles associated with Ronald Knapp's Gorby 2 career and the Gorbachev visit in December of 1988.

Reprinted on United Press International, Sunday, December 11, 1988:

Los Angeles Times

December 4, 1987

"In Turning it Around, You Might Say Gorbachev Looks Like Ronald Knapp: He Could Cause Tremblin in the Kremlin"

By: Claudia Luther

It couldn't be, could it? Is that Mikhail S. Gorbachev, Soviet leader and architect of Glasnost and Perestroika, on the dance floor doing the twist?

"I can go lower than anyone else in town," he boasts. "I'm serious! The young guys can't believe this gray-haired guy."

That's right. It's not really Gorbachev. Ronald V. Knapp of Huntington Beach, a commercial real estate broker and all around fun guy, is almost a dead ringer for the Soviet leader with the help of a little fingernail polish, and he has decided to make the best of the resemblance.

* * *

Knapp, whose 5/9-foot, 185-pound frame has the chunky look, said a friend accused him of belonging to the Communist Party, joking that he had seen Knapp's picture on the front page of the Times.

He's even learning Russian

Knapp has been teaching himself Russian with audiotapes as he jogs on the beach, just in case he ever gets to talk to some real Russians. Among the words he has learned is *zamir* - peace.

Knapp, a resident of Huntington Beach for 24 years and a graduate of Cal State Fullerton, is particularly proud of having played Santa Claus every year for the last 17 years at St. Bonaventure Church in Huntington Beach.

He has worked with American Indians for the Ocean View School District in Huntington Beach, was a senior engineer at McDonnell Douglas in Long Beach, and was once in the commercial Christmas tree business and had a truck firm on Beach Boulevard for a time. He even ran for Huntington Beach City Council in 1970 and lost.

I've got so many dents in my fender, you wouldn't believe it, " Knapp said.

In the meantime, he has raised his children: Teresa, 24; Patrick, 22; Connie, 18; Jim, 19; and Shawn,17.

How do they feel about their father's new persona?

"They roll their eyebrows," Knapp said. "They're not quite sure about their old man anymore. They think he's gone over the hill, and no telling what he'll do now."

The article featured these photos:

Featured Photos by Aurelio Jose Barrera in the *Los Angeles Times*:

Ronald V. Knapp preparing to take a sip of Russian spirits, is hailed as a pretty close look-alike to Soviet leader Mikhail S. Gorbachev. December 4, 1987

Pre-summit harmony - It's not really Reagan and Gorbachev, just impersonators Jay Koch as the President and Ronald Knapp as his Soviet counterpart. Knapp won a nationwide Gorbachev look-alike search.

Washington Post, December 7, 1988

"Soviets Said to Plan Major Military Cut; Leader's Arrival Stirs New York"

Byline: Howard Kurtz

...Descending from an Aeroflot jet with his wife, Raisa, after a 10-hour flight from Moscow, Gorbachev extended greeting to the United Nations, the American people and "all New Yorkers" and expressed high hopes for his meeting Wednesday with President Reagan and President-elect George Bush.

The start of the three-day visit had an even greater impact on New York traffic, as police closed three major highways to the Triborough Bridge, enabling the Gorbachev motorcade to whisk from John F. Kennedy International Airport to the Soviet Mission.

Outside the mission, several hundred police officers, part of a 6,600-member contingent assigned to the Gorbachev visit, blocked streets, kept pedestrians moving and surveyed the scene from rooftops and fire escapes. Several blocks around the East 67th Street building were declared a "frozen" zone.

Several reporters were fooled by a Gorbachev look-alike, Ronald Knapp, whose efforts to promote a television show included fake journalists shouting, "There he is! There he is!"

United Press International

December 7 1988

"Gorby Impostor Meets Trump"

By: Gerry Mullany

Dateline: New York

A Mikhail Gorbachev look-alike stunned pedestrians in Midtown Manhattan Tuesday and even got to meet the king of capitalism—Donald Trump—who wished the communist pretender well in his travels through New York.

The impostor drew hundreds of gawkers who did not expect to see the balding Soviet comrade stroll down Times Square to mingle with the working folk.

As the Gorby look-alike traveled through Midtown in a limousine, the real Gorbachev was arriving at Kennedy International Airport in Queens for the first day of a visit to New York that will end Friday.

Gordon Elliott, a freelance television producer, said he came up with the idea for the Gorbachev impostor to see how jaded New Yorkers would take to the charismatic Soviet leader.

The reaction was incredible," he said. "Ninety-nine percent of the people thought it was true."

After greeting people in Times Square, the Gorbachev look-alike showed up at Trump Tower, a bastion of capitalism, and caused enough of a stir to draw the building's owner down to the street.

A filming of the meeting broadcast on the television program *A Current Affair* showed the Gorbachev impostor needling Trump about his red tie.

Although Elliott said Trump "was absolutely taken" by the impostor, a spokesman for the real estate baron denied the savvy capitalist was duped.

The Gorbachev impostor was actually Ronald Knapp, an American Indian who bears an uncanny resemblance to the Soviet leader, Elliott said.

Los Angeles Times

December 7, 1988

"New York Bids Gorbachevs a Grumpy Hello"

John J. Goldman and Bob Drogin

Guarded by scores of police and security agents, surrounded by a hundred reporters and flanked by television trucks and satellite dishes, an ordinary city block on the East Side of Manhattan suddenly became a tightly guarded diplomatic compound - to the inconvenience and discomfort of many of its regular residents.

As the motorcade crossed the final intersection of East 67th Street and Third Avenue, Raisa Gorbachev waved a gloved hand at the reporters and photographers.

With little else to shoot, the cameras quickly crowded around Ronald V. Knapp of Huntington Beach, Calif., a pudgy, balding man who looks a lot like Gorbachev thanks to a carefully applied stain on his forehead. In case anyone should miss the point, he also gave out cards of his picture on which he had signed Gorbachev's name.

Attached photo to article:

Photo: Ronald Knapp, a Gorbachev imitator, poses for a portrait outside the Soviet Mission.

Associated Press

Dec. 7, 1988

Police, Demonstrators, Bystanders in Gorby's Neighborhood

NEW YORK (AP)__ Hundreds of police who sealed off the Soviet Mission for Mikhail Gorbachev's visit didn't deter protesters or other bystanders, including a "Gorby" look-alike who briefly fooled the media and Donald Trump.

When the real Soviet leader arrived Tuesday at the mission on Manhattan's fashionable Upper East Side, he waved from his limousine to the crowds. The car then disappeared into a ramp to an underground garage.

But 30 minutes before Gorbachev's arrival, Ronald V. Knapp caused a bigger commotion among the hundreds of people milling through nearby streets.

Knapp, the spitting image of Gorbachev down to what looked like a wine-colored birthmark on his head, drove up a block away from the mission in a silver stretch limousine. As confused media members scrambled for their cameras and notepads, Knapp stood on the corner speaking through an interpreter. . . .

* * *

When Knapp strolled past Tiffany's in midafternoon greeting shoppers with a Russian-sounding "Hi," hundreds crowded around – perhaps remembering the

Soviet leader's impromptu appearance on a Washington, D.C, street during last year's summit,

The impersonator's act was apparently good enough to fool real estate tycoon Donald Trump, who recently learned that Gorbachev had turned down a chance to visit the developer's glittering Trump Tower.

Trump, accompanied by bodyguards, rushed down from his nearby office and pushed his way through the crowd for a chance to pump the hand of the world leader.

"He looked fabulous and he sounded fabulous, but I knew it couldn't be right," Trump said. "For one thing, I looked into the back of his limo and saw four very attractive women. I knew that his society had not come that far yet in terms of capitalist decadence."

Associated Press

December 6, 1988

Waiting for Gorby: Law, Locals, Look-Alike

NEW YORK(AP) . . . Hundreds of police officers stood on the streets and roofs surrounding the mission, where the Soviet leader is staying during his two-day visit, as an assortment of the curious and media conscious milled among them.

Gorbachev finally pulled up shortly before 4 p.m., waving at the crowd as his 45-car motorcade streamed through Manhattan's East Side.

Ronald V Knapp, however, arrived about a half hour earlier.

Knapp, the spitting image of the Soviet leader down to what looked like a birthmark on his head, drove up a block away from the mission in a silver stretch limousine. As confused media members scrambled for their cameras and notepads, Knapp stood on the corner speaking through an interpreter.

The New York Times

The Gorbachev Visit; Manhattan Goes Gorbachev, From Fish to Oreo Cookies

By Maureen Dowd

Published December 07, 1988

. . . Gorbachev is known for having an unpredictable streak. So when a man who looked just like the Soviet leader strolled past Tiffany's at 1 P.M. yesterday and began greeting shoppers with a Russian-sounding "Hi," hundreds of shoppers on Fifth Avenue crowded around eagerly.

This was the world leader, after all, who suddenly jumped out of his limousine on a downtown corner in Washington last year to shake hands with surprised passers-by.

Donald Trump, hearing that Mr. Gorbachev was in front of Trump Tower, rushed down from his office to see if the Communist leader had changed his mind back about viewing the Manhattan billionaire's lush capitalist empire.

Mr. Trump and his bodyguards wedged their way through the crowd and shook hands with the man who was a dead ringer for Mr. Gorbachev—right down to the distinctive mark on his scalp.

As it turned out it was not the Soviet leader at all, but an actor named Ronald V. Knapp, the winner of a Gorbachev look-alike contest. Mr. Knapp was meandering around New York, from Fifth Avenue to the Soviet Mission to Bloomingdale's, being filmed by television crews from Channel 5.

Gordon Elliott, who is the host for several Channel 5 programs and who accompanied Mr. Knapp in his charade, said afterward that Mr. Trump had fallen for the gag. "There was absolutely no question that he bought it," Mr. Elliott said.

Mr. Trump said that, once he got close up, he knew immediately that it was not the Soviet leader – especially since the pretender did not allude to the previous time the two had met and treated the deal -making mogul as a stranger.

www.ingramcontent.com/pod-product-compliance
Lightning Source LLC
Chambersburg PA
CBHW071528040426
42452CB00008B/926